PHILADELPHIA: BEYOND THE LIBERTY BELL

PHILADELPHIA: BEYOND THE LIBERTY BELL

A GUIDE TO THE LITTLE-KNOWN, HIDDEN TREASURES OF THE DELAWARE VALLEY

BY RON AVERY

PHOTOGRAPHY BY HINDA SCHUMAN
FOREWORD BY MARCIAROSE SHESTACK

BROAD STREET BOOKS
PHILADELPHIA

Cover design by Robin Fogel
Cover illustration by Fred Birchman

This book is catalogued at the Library of Congress as
Philadelphia: Beyond the Liberty Bell: 91-072050
ISBN: 1-879174-02-2

PRINTED IN THE UNITED STATES OF AMERICA

TABLE OF CONTENTS
PHILADELPHIA: BEYOND THE LIBERTY BELL

FOREWORD

I' m a Philaphile,
I love Philadelphia,
And I didn't think I would.

I came here by way of New York, Boston, Chicago and Baton Rouge, LA, because in my still-green youth I married a Philadelphia lawyer.

He assured me I would love Philadelphia.

. . . I yearned for L.A.

He told me that no other city in America could boast such extraordinary suburbs as close to the city as Philadelphia.

. . . I dreamt of Washington, D.C.

He assured me that as a history buff I would get goose bumps walking down the very streets that were trod by Jefferson, Madison and Franklin.

. . . I pined for Chicago.

So we came to Philadelphia.

But, we had an agreement that only a really smart Philadelphia lawyer could have devised. He said, "If at the end of one year you're not happy here, I promise, regardless of my job opportunities, we will leave." It looked like he was taking a big risk. He sounded like a truly caring and devoted spouse. But he understood that he wasn't really placing his burgeoning career in jeopardy because he knew his city.

Before the end of the year I was hooked.

. . . And I have been ever since.

Philadelphia is a city of extraordinary grace and charm and scale. It is the fourth-largest city in America, but its center city is totally encompassable. It has parks and rivers and theater and ballet and the Philadelphia Orchestra. It has museums and galleries and restaurants and vibrant nightclubs where young people cavort on man-made beaches along the Delaware River.

It is a city of quiet Quaker legacy and Main Line patrician elite. At the same time the energy of its neighborhoods is blatantly, chauvinistically, devotedly ethnic. Philadelphia cherishes the old and preserves it. But it creates the new and heralds it. Even as the city hallows its Colonial tradition, it creates a dazzling contemporary skyline.

Rivaling Boston, it has more than 80 institutions of higher learning, great teaching hospitals and a thriving health-care and pharmaceutical industry, as well as a biotech corridor and centers of banking, finance and law. It is a gracious, appealing and uniquely manageable city.

Okay, Okay, Okay. So I love Philadelphia.

The point of this preface is that Ron Avery does too. And he has written a wonderfully engaging and beguiling book that takes you beyond the obvious "must-sees" of Philadelphia to out-of-the-way, quirky, curious and fascinating places most Philadelphians don't even know exist.

Now you should understand that this fellow Avery is the gen–u–ine Philadelphia article. He can write about his city because he has a unique handle on it. As a working newspaperman he has been covering this area for more than 25 years. Need more proof? He was born in a Philadelphia rowhouse and he still lives in one today.

For the last eight years, Ron Avery has worked at the *Philadelphia Daily News*, mostly writing features on interesting places and people in Philadelphia. His knowledge of the city, however, is not merely encyclopedic; it is also offbeat, irreverent and delightfully open to the bizarre, the outlandish and the uncommon.

In this book, Ron assumes you've been to the Art Museum and climbed Rocky's steps, seen where Betsy Ross sewed the first flag, and of course, as the book's title suggests — touched the crack in the Liberty Bell. The guidebook is particularly for the curious Philadelphian who knows the obvious sites of his city — and is ready to explore the unknown and the unexpected.

Ron's is the road less traveled. And what intriguing journeys he suggests. He takes you to a concrete castle built by a cantankerous eccentric, to an elegant French mansion that became the preserve of a black religious cult figure, to a bizarre museum devoted to death and mourning, and to a Civil War museum that boasts a shingle from Grant's cabin at Appomattox and a brick from Lincoln's box at Ford's Theater.

Avery wants it understood that not every place he chronicles will be one that you will necessarily want to visit. But all the places have stories you will find engaging, enlightening and sometimes amazing. That's because Ron Avery brings to his subject matter not only the reporter's craft, but the history buff's love of the arcane.

He is a spirited writer whose wit and style carry you up stairs, around corners, under eaves and down labyrinthine passageways all in the quest of surprise and discovery right in your own Philadelphia backyard.

The good news is that Ron Avery has chronicled more than 50 fascinating places to explore in or about Philadelphia. The even better news is that he has so much Philadelphia information stored away, there is sure to be a sequel!

Marciarose Shestack

July 4, 1991
Philadelphia . . . of course

PHILADELPHIA:
BEYOND THE LIBERTY BELL

William Wagner: merchant, scientist, philanthropist.

Chapter 1

A MUSEUM THAT FOSSILIZED
Wagner Free Institute of Science

More than any other place the forgotten Wagner Free Institute of Science in North Philadelphia inspired the writing of this book.

Serenely slumbering in what today is a depressed, depopulated area, Wagner is the ultimate example of a Philadelphia institution that totters along on pure inertia. In any other city it would have been declared an anachronism decades ago and promptly bulldozed. It has been a museum virtually without visitors, an educational institution without students.

But it is also a perfectly preserved historic gem. That Philadelphia propensity to do nothing has created at the Wagner Institute a perfect time capsule.

This tradition of clinging to institutions long after they outlive any apparent usefulness is one reason Philadelphia is so rich in the odd and the interesting.

Perhaps no other metropolitian area in the nation has so many institutions, small museums, unheralded historic sites, social clubs, associations and intriguing oddities of every sort.

Benjamin Franklin set the trend, and scores of Philadelphians have since established or endowed a school, museum, hospital, library, art gallery, memorial, even a playground.

Philadelphians are also champions at forming clubs and organizations. In 1732, twenty-seven fishing buddies created a fishing and gourmet eatin' club. The "State In Schuylkill," or Fish House, is still meeting and eating. Philadelphians with a passion for dancing started a Dancing Assembly in 1748. The Assembly is still dancing away. A volunteer cavalry unit mounted up in 1775. More than two centuries later the First City Troop is still galloping along.

The region, too, has a tradition of nurturing the nonconformist, the creative eccentric. And so today we can visit the castle of Henry Mercer, the mansion of Father Divine, the Ryerss family pet cemetery and the urban log cabin of Joyce and Jeff Thomas.

Whatever the causes, the Delaware Valley is a region rich in small gems – interesting little-known nuggets worth visiting, worth knowing about.

Which brings us back to the mean streets of North Philadelphia and Wagner Free Institute of Science.

Step inside this nearly block-long edifice and enter the 19th century. If the ghost of William Wagner were to wander upstairs from his basement burial crypt, he would find everything just the way he left it at the time of his demise in 1885. OK, they have installed electric lights.

Wagner was a wealthy import-export merchant who learned his trade under the tutelage of Stephen Girard. He was also a gentleman–scientist of great accomplishment and an enthusiastic collector of minerals, fossils, stuffed animals, birds eggs, shells, bones and any other oddities he could buy or find. Wagner made his fortune by age 44 and retired to travel, build his collection and dabble in science.

In the late 1840s he began giving free science lectures at his home. By 1855 he chartered a school, hired a faculty and offered free courses in a municipal building. Wagner's noble goal was to bring the amazing new strides in understanding the world through science to the average man.

In 1860, Wagner started construction on the Institute next to his estate, Elm Grove. It was suburban pasture at the time. The architect for the Greek Revival building was John McArthur Jr., the same man responsible for Philadelphia City Hall and many other 19th century public buildings. The Institute opened its doors in 1865, and since this was low-key Philadelphia there was no fanfare. Keeping a low profile has become ingrained at the Institute.

It's a huge place and very impressive once you get inside. The largest component is the cavernous museum. Its handsome, old display cases house some 23,000 items.

The bulk of the specimens was collected or purchased by Wagner. Natural lighting is provided by 25-foot-high windows. There are two levels of galleries overlooking the main display area.

Chances are any visitor will have the place to himself, providing an odd feeling of being alone in another century. That odd sensation becomes even stronger as soon as you enter the 600-seat lecture hall. It's an old-fashioned amphitheater – much like the one shown in the Thomas Eakins' painting of the "Gross Clinic" depicting medical students watching surgery.

Under each chair is a wire rack for stowing a high silk hat. It takes only the slightest bit of imagination to visualize that lecture hall filled with 19th century gentlemen in period garb listening to Professor Wagner discoursing on the new concept of evolution.

The Institute's handsome library once contained 25,000 volumes. Many of those books are rare early scientific works, and most have been lent to local universities or specialized libraries.

When Wagner died he was entombed in the unpretentious basement crypt. But a year later his wife had the body removed to a more conventional resting place at West Laurel Hill Cemetery in Bala Cynwyd. It was only recently that the staff investigated that forgotten – but not empty – crypt. To the delight of local historians, the tomb contained numerous sea chests brimming with fascinating reading. The find included all of Wagner's business papers, dating to 1819, his science lecture-notes and correspondence with noted scientists and explorers of his time. During the Institute's early years, all the city's top scientists were associated with it. The most notable was Joseph Leidy, whose statue stands outside the Academy of Natural Sciences.

Inside the Institute: bones and long rows of display cases.

The Wagner Free Institute of Science was designed by John McArthur Jr., architect of Philadelphia City Hall.

Wagner Institute display cases have not been touched in more than a century.

Leidy, president of the Academy and chairman of the department of anatomy at the University of Pennsylvania, became the Institute's director in 1885. The Institute was fairly active at this point, sending out fossil-hunting expeditions that added 100 "type" fossils to the collection. A "type" specimen is a new animal or plant never before recorded by science. It becomes the standard for comparing other finds. Among those finds was the first sabertooth tiger, whose dusty bones are still in the same display case.

The entire museum is just the way Leidy laid it out more than 100 years ago. Nothing has been changed. The handwritten labels on each object are the originals.

The Wagner Institute's great value today is being "a museum of a museum." Other museums from the Victorian era do survive, but at least they have changed the displays a bit, added some new stuff. Not at Wagner.

William Wagner left his institute a $2 million endowment – just enough to keep it alive but fortunately not enough to modernize the place. A nephew of the childless Wagner took over as head of the seven-member board, and that hasn't changed either. Wagner descendants still dominate the board, a family obligation passed from father to son.

When the Institute was more active, many famous scientists came to lecture, including Margaret Mead and John Dewey. Its free science courses were popular into the 1930s. But by the 1960s few people were willing to come into the neighborhood at night, and the courses are now given at several branch libraries around the city.

Except for class trips, there are few visitors. Those who do venture down nearly always register amazement. How has it survived so long, so unchanged, so unaffected by time?

The Wagner Institute is located at 17th and Montgomery. Opened Tuesday through Friday. 9 a.m. to 4 p.m. and Saturday by appointment. Best to call ahead. Phone: 763-6529

✳ ✳ ✳ ✳ ✳

Chapter 2

THE FATHER, MOTHER
AND A HECK OF A MANSION
Woodmont Mansion

In the wonderful, whacky world of American religious cult figures, the late Father Divine was a giant. Unlike competing Gantryesque windbags who merely claimed to speak for God, the Father claimed he was God.

Unlike some oily charlatans who accumulated wealth by impoverishing gullible believers, Father Divine amassed vast wealth and shared it with a host of humble followers.

The Father gave up his "bodily form in the likeness of man," and/or died in 1965. Meanwhile his wife, known as Mother Divine, and a staff of aging followers enjoy a delicious helping of heaven on earth in a fabulously opulent Main Line mansion known as Woodmont.

Woodmont is an eye-popping French Gothic-style, 32-room mansion situated on 73 acres of manicured lawns, formal gardens and woodland in Gladwyne.

MARILYN A. SHAPIRO
Woodmont: a masterpiece of French Gothic architecture.

Built by steel baron Alan Wood Jr. in 1892, it's a prime example of the "Age of Elegance" that can match a lot of the biggies along millionaires' row in Newport, Rhode Island. It cost Wood $1 million to build Woodmont a century ago. It's hard to even guess today's market value.

A few yards from the castle-like mansion, Father Divine is entombed in a massive granite mausoleum called "The Shrine of Life." The grounds, the shrine and the first floor of the mansion are open free of charge to visitors Sunday afternoons from April through October. It's something that shouldn't be missed.

"The International Code of Modesty" posted in the parking lot warns against drinking, smoking, profanity or undue mixing of the sexes. In practical terms: don't wear shorts. But women who do arrive in shorts are provided with a wraparound skirt.

The Great Hall of Woodmont is rich in fine woods, fine art and opulent furnishings.

MARILYN A. SHAPIRO

The first room in the guided tour of the mansion is the "Great Hall," which lies under a 45-foot-high oak ceiling supported by flying buttresses. Throughout the mansion are magnificent fireplaces, oriental carpets, expensive oil paintings – of the Old-Masters variety – and quality antique furniture.

The tour includes Father Divine's oak-paneled study, a library done in rose mahogany, the solarium and music room.

The dining room with its elaborately carved oak panels and massive table set with the most exquisite china, crystal, silver and linen is the most impressive and opulent room on the tour.

Mother Divine, a tall, dignified woman, born Edna Rose Ritchings, took the name Sweet Angel after becoming a follower of the Father in the 1940s; she can often be seen in the mansion on Sundays when elaborate formal dinner parties are held. Guests who cannot be accommodated in the dining room can observe the main party over closed-circuit television.

There is always a place left at the head of the table for Father Divine. His old lectures are re-read again by Mother Divine at dinners and other functions. The cult's newspaper, "The New Day" endlessly reprints his old addresses.

Asked about the feasting and lavishness of Woodmont, Mother Divine says, "We don't own this as individuals. We share in the beauty. Woodmont demonstrates God's abundance. Father stressed visualizing what you want to materialize. You too can enjoy such as this." Explaining the communal feasts, she said, "Father is Jesus returned. It's just natural that he would feed the people."

The sect never actively proselytizes, but the visitor gets an overdose of the sect's philosophy at the Shrine of Life. The massive brass doors to the tomb are covered with carvings of figures that symbolize principles taught by Father Divine. Guides present a long-winded sermon on each symbol.

Inside, the body lies under massive slabs of polished red granite referred to as the "ark of the covenant." Two large, bronze angels kneel in prayer on top of the ark. The roof of the shrine is a pyramid, lined on the inside with scores of gold-leaf tiles from Japan.

MARILYN A. SHAPIRO

The entire dining room of Woodmont, including wall panels, was imported from England.

Followers greet each other, and visitors, with the word "Peace," and it is hard to imagine more tranquil, peaceful folks. Most are quite elderly. Celibacy is the iron rule in this faith, so there's not much young blood around. (Father

Woodmont cost $1 million when it was built by steel magnate Alan Wood Jr. in 1892.

MARILYN A. SHAPIRO

Divine's marriage to Mother Divine was strictly spiritual.)

His origins are shrouded in mystery. He was probably born in Georgia shortly after the Civil War. He started his Peace Mission Movement in Harlem about 1915. The movement reached its apex during the Depression when Father Divine did, indeed, become a savior to thousands of poor urban blacks and down-and-out whites.

His business savvy created a solid real estate and business empire operated on communal principles. Followers worked in Peace Mission hotels, dry cleaners, gas stations, barbershops and cafeterias. As long as they lived according to the Movement's tenets, their needs were secure. Historians say Father Divine was an important and effective figure in the struggle for racial equality in the 1930s and 1940s.

Woodmont is open to the public Sundays from 1 p.m. to 5 p.m. April through October. Take the Schuylkill Expressway to Conshohocken Exit 29. Take Route 23 East, left at first traffic light, Spring Mill Road. Go a few blocks to Woodmont Road, across from golf course, and make left. Woodmont is on the right at the double iron gate.

* * * * *

MARILYN A. SHAPIR

The Shrine of Life "in which the body of God is enshrined," according to the followers of Father Divine.

Chapter 3

MATTERS OF
GRAVE CONCERN

It was that smirking wiseacre H.L. Mencken – a native of Baltimore, of all places – who described Philadelphia as a "well-lighted cemetery." Well, Philadelphia does have many delightful cemeteries. The Colonial burial grounds of Old Swedes' Church, Christ Church and Mikveh Israel Synagogue are marvelous pockets of restful tranquility and historical interest.

In this chapter we'll take a respectful stroll through three other Philadelphia area cemeteries of note.

ARLINGTON CEMETERY'S
MUSEUM OF MOURNING ART

Deadly but not boring, here is a museum concerned solely with death and mourning. It is believed to be the only museum in the nation dedicated entirely to these dark themes. It opened in 1990 in an otherwise unremarkable Delaware County cemetery.

Perhaps because our ancestors did a lot more dying – and a lot sooner – they invested a great deal of thought and effort in the processes of death and mourning. They read instruction manuals on proper dying. They surrounded death with symbolism, poetry, special clothing, art and jewelry.

Housed in a newly opened office/chapel building, which is modeled on George Washington's home at Mount Vernon, the museum displays all the paraphernalia of death. Professionally organized with plenty of explanatory notes, it offers a rather fascinating glimpse into the area of behavior and ritual which most history books totally neglect.

The displays demonstrate the gradual change in attitudes toward death from the stark symbolism of the skull and bones, judgment and hell-fire of the Middle Ages to the sentimentality of the Victorian era with its gentle lambs, willows and rosebuds.

Death had its own literature. Best-sellers on display here include "The Rules and Exercises of Holy Dying" and "Fears of Death With Seasonal Directions on how to Prepare Ourselves to Die Well." The museum offers many examples of elegiac poetry, printed

A horse-drawn hearse and cemetery fence at the Museum of Mourning Art.

eulogies, sermons (once popular reading) and even a novel published in 1782 titled "Dead to the Living."

One section is devoted to the death of George Washington, whose passing unleashed a flood of sentimental artifacts and collectibles that may have stood unmatched until the untimely passing of Elvis.

There are displays of black mourning clothes. A death bell and a bill from the bellringer are displayed next to a shiny, black horse-drawn hearse.

The custom of willing money for the purchase of mourning rings and other jewelry stems from an era when people want-

Arlington Cemetery's Museum of Mourning Art is part of this replica of Mount Vernon.

ed a maximum number of mourners to pray for their soul. The bribe of a ring, brooch or new mourning clothes helped insure a crowd. A letter written by a Colonial preacher says he has "a quart tankard filled with mourning rings." The museum displays a complete line of such jewelry. Memorializing a life in needlework was very popular, and there are many examples of this folk art in the museum.

Curator Anita Schorsch or an assistant will provide free, fact-filled tours of the museum for individuals or groups by appointment. It's all very educational, and afterward you can impress friends with your knowledgeable comments on "hatchments", "mourning ivories", and "consolation literature."

The Mourning Art Museum, a building modeled on Mount Vernon, is at Arlington Cemetery, Lansdowne Avenue and State Road, Drexel Hill. Call for an appointment. Phone: 259-3184

PALMER BURIAL GROUND

There are few places in the city which provide such a strong feeling of timeless continuity as this leafy burial ground in old Fishtown.

In 1732 the sea captain Anthony Palmer put aside five and a half acres as a free burial ground for all residents of what was then called The Kensington District of the Northern Liberties.

Generation-after-generation of Fishtowners come together in death in this peaceful spot in the heart of their close-knit community. No one knows for sure how many are buried here; a fire in the cemetery office in 1878 destroyed early records. A conservative estimate is 20,000 burials since Colonial days. Every year a dozen or more Fishtowners join their neighbors. The only requirement is Fishtown residency. The only charge, a modest fee for the gravediggers.

There is a moving poignancy about the place. This was always a working class enclave. Its first residents worked on the docks and in the shipyards. They were artisans and laborers with large families. Now, as in the past, there may be no money for a proper tombstone. A dozen recent burials are marked by simple handmade wooden crosses. Sometimes a painted rock indicates the grave of a family member, or a cinderblock is sunk into the

One of the newer burials at Fishtown's old Palmer Burial Ground.

ground with only the top showing for the bereaved family to paint a name or date on. Inexpensive metal markers are common; so are graves decorated with plastic flowers and small trinkets.

A particularly sad monument at Laurel Hill Cemetery marks the grave of a mother and her twin children.

In time, the wooden crosses and homemade markers disappear. The acid soil eventually destroys a wood coffin. Dust to dust. Space is created for another generation of burials. All graves are hand-dug so as not to destroy unmarked and forgotten burials.

The old tombstones reveal the horrendous death rate for children in past centuries. The four children of Hiram and Martha Carlton lie together under one tombstone, victims of some deadly epidemic in 1864. Christine Durr died in 1777 at age 37. Her tombstone reveals that she was buried in the same grave as three of her infant children.

Veterans of every war from the Revolution to Vietnam are buried here. Some family names appear again and again. The cemetery is the final resting place for one Seminole Indian and several Spaniards. No one remembers what brought these strangers to Fishtown.

A neighborhood committee operates the graveyard, sponsoring flea markets to raise funds for its upkeep. Vandalism does occur, but not very often. Practically everyone in the area has some family member or ancestor buried here.

The cemetery is surrounded by houses that are a century or two old. A small building called "The Bier House" dates to 1875 and was designed by the architectural firm of Frank Furness. An old wooden bier hangs in one corner. It was charred and blackened in the fire of 1878.

The feeling of continuity, generation-linked-to-generation is extraordinary.

Palmer Burial Ground is at Palmer and Belgrade Streets.

LAUREL HILL
CEMETERY

A city guidebook published in 1847 recommends Laurel Hill to the visiting tourist as "the largest and most beautiful cemetery near Philadelphia. . . . Its surface is extremely undulating, beautified with numerous forest and ornamental trees. . . . (it) contains many beautiful monuments as well as the mortal remains of many distinguished personages."

For reasons perhaps social historians can explain, our 19th century ancestors suddenly decided the simple church graveyard and modest headstones were out. Soaring monuments, fancy statuary and landscaping to rival the gardens at Versailles were in.

Laurel Hill, which opened in 1836, was among the nation's first and grandest of the new parklike American cemeteries. They weren't just parklike, these gardens of the dead were actual parks. Families arrived toting picnic baskets and spent the day. Sundays were so mobbed, the cemetery started issuing tickets. Handsome guidebooks were published for visitors; there were occasional band concerts.

Laurel Hill remains a splendid artifact that reveals a great deal about Victorian attitudes and thinking. There are history professors who take their classes to see the place. The cemetery has a volunteer "friends" group, which sponsors tours and publishes an interesting and readable newsletter.

For some Laurel Hillniks the allure comes from the names on its monuments, a veritable Who's Who of important Philadelphia families and personalities. Countless generals, admirals, mayors, millionaires, authors, Arctic explorers and captains of industry are buried here. For other cemetery devotees, the fun comes from exploration and discovery.

According to some lurid accounts, the canny entrepreneurs who founded the cemetery needed an important corpse to bring in burials of other bigshots. They practically resorted to grave robbery to get the cadaver of Charles Thomson, secretary of the First and Second Continental Congresses, transferred from a church cemetery to Laurel Hill. The Thomson caper still stirs passions and debate among historians and certain bluebloods.

Modern cemeteries tend to be a monotonous sea of uniform stones, crosses or ground-level markers, all lined up in even ranks for easy grass mowing. Laurel Hill, on the other hand, is mazelike and hilly. In fact, it once employed a shepherd and kept a flock of sheep to trim the grass. Its monuments are characterized by variety, creativity, individuality and sentimentality. It's really a sculpture garden: a forest of looming obelisks, Greek-temple mausoleums, odd statues and stone crypts festooned with doodads and decorative detail.

The cemetery covers a full 95 acres overlooking the Schuylkill. There have been about 80,000 burials, and about 100 newcomers are planted each year.

Among the more interesting monuments is the statue of a woman holding two children in her arms as she looks toward the Schuylkill. The monument marks the grave of a woman and her twin toddlers who drowned in a boat accident on the river.

A strange five-sided memorial marks the grave of a late 19th century spiritualist. Carved on the tomb is virtually her entire curriculum vitae (including address) and statements concerning her philosphy.

It was an era of symbolism. The monument of a young soldier who died with Custer at the Little Big Horn is a broken column decorated with a glove, a hat and spurs. Another monument, designed by Alexander Stirling Calder, portrays a ghost slipping out of a half-opened sarcophagus.

The entrance to Laurel Cemetery is the gatehouse on the 3200 block of Ridge Avenue. Call the Friends of Laurel Hill Cemetery for tour information. Phone: 228-8817

✳ ✳ ✳ ✳

Chapter 4

THE ADDAMS FAMILY
DOESN'T LIVE HERE ANYMORE
Ebeneezer Maxwell Mansion

Imagine the house that was the inspiation for the creepy old mansion haunted by television's cornball spooks "The Addams Family!"

Sorry to disappoint you. This isn't it. The rumor started years ago, and it kind of stuck. Many still call this Germantown classic "the Addams House," and it seems believable. For one, Charles Addams, whose macabre cartoons in the New Yorker inspired the TV show, attended the University of Pennsylvania. He may have seen the Maxwell Mansion when it was abandoned, forbidding and spooky.

While there's no evidence to support this theory, any ghoul or vampire looking for a place to chain-up for the night would find the Ebeneezer Maxwell Mansion prime real estate.

While there are no ghost stories attached to the property, there is an interesting saga of how this dandy diamond of a house was rescued from the jaws of demolition and preserved as a museum.

The house was built in 1859 as a sort of speculative investment when Germantown was the suburb of choice for upwardly mobile Philadelphians. Maxwell was a dry-goods merchant who apparently married into money when he got hitched to Anna Smith, his second cousin. The couple and their six kids lived in the new house for about two years. Maxwell sold it at a profit to businessman William Hunter. Hunter's daughter, Augusta Rosalie Stevenson, inherited the grand house and lived there until her death in 1956. A lot of people still remember "Gussie," who married several times and traveled a lot but never had children.

Gussie's heirs wanted to unload the place. In the mid-1950s, 18-room Victorian mansions were very un-hip. There were no takers, but fuel oil dealer Isadore Kirschner thought the corner location would be good for a gas station. He was just about to close a $35,000 deal, pending a zoning change, when neighbors got wind of it.

There was a community meeting, and a posse of irate Germantowners went to the zoning hearing to oppose a gas station on the residential block. The zoning was denied

Gracious Victorian living at the Ebenezer Maxwell Mansion in Germantown.

and the mansion saved – for the time being. Six months later the house was put up at auction. Kirschner came out of curiosity and, finding no serious bidders, decided to pick it up for $19,000.

For a while it was rented to a woman who operated a foster home. But in 1964, Kirschner found a buyer. The retirement home next door wanted to expand and needed the land, but the mansion would have to go.

A public-spirited neighbor with connections at the Historical Commission got wind of the sale just in time; the retirement home already had its demolition permit. But within four days of the application, historical certification was granted – certainly a speed record for city government.

This provided a six-month reprieve for the mansion, but it was too late for an old stone stable, which was demolished. Six months later by a margin of one vote, the board of directors of the retirement home agreed to lease the mansion to the Germantown Historical Society, saving it once more from the bulldozers. In 1976, a new non-profit corporation managed to buy the mansion and started the long, painstaking renovations and furnishing process.

While there are a number of Colonial homes open to the public in Germantown, the Maxwell Mansion is the lone Victorian-era dwelling. It's a classic, combining many architectural styles. Through private fund raising and charitable grants it has been restored and re-furnished with extraordinary care to insure authenticity.

Fortunately both Maxwell and Hunter left detailed inventories of the house and its furnishings, providing accurate guides for the restorers. Heirs of the Maxwells have

An authentic 19th century Victorian kitchen with all the old utensils.

The dining room is set for high tea inside the Maxwell Mansion.

donated some items of family furniture plus photo portraits of Ebeneezer and Anna. All other funishings are from the period with many items coming from other Germantown mansions.

One interesting and challenging aspect of the renovation job was duplicating the original finishes on wood and stone. All the woodwork was originally stained and "grained" to make it look like more expensive woods. Slate fireplaces were grained to look like marble. Wood window frames were "sand painted" a technique that makes wood look like stone.

Colorful painted design patterns have been restored to walls and door panels. The wallpaper and rugs may be new, but they are exact duplicates of patterns popular in such 19th century houses. The committee spent a year trying to get the curtains and window treatments just right.

The mania for authenticity is demonstrated in the research that went into re-pointing the exterior stone walls. A thorough search revealed one section of wall which had never been retouched. The mortar was chemically analyzed, and the exact formula reproduced.

Antiques-buffs will go ga-ga over the furniture. In fact, *Antiques Magazine* did a six-page spread on the place. There's a lot of furniture.

The dining room is particularly plush. A huge carved mahogany bed and matching washstand in the master bedroom are spectacular.

The child's bedroom is particularly appealing, with its games, dollhouse and period toys. The kitchen is reminiscent of the place Mrs. Bridges labored in, in the television series "Upstairs Downstairs." In fact, there is a rear stair off the kitchen leading to the servants' quarters. Along with the big iron stove, period sink and icebox, the room contains many culinary gadgets of the era: a sausage stuffer, cherry pitter, apple corer/peeler and lemon juice squeezer.

Outdoors, great labor and caring have been invested in the creation of Victorian-era gardens. There are a grape arbor, climbing roses on the porch, a tiny pond and two hemlocks bent into an arch.

The entire mansion is a wonderful time capsule. Every Christmas the volunteers deck the place out for "a Dickens Christmas" and in the summer there's a gala "Ice Cream Social."

The Ebeneezer Maxwell Mansion, Greene and Tulpehocken Streets. Open Wednesday through Sunday, 1 p.m. to 5 p.m. Phone: 438-1861

✳ ✳ ✳ ✳ ✳

Chapter 5

TWO REASONS TO TRAVEL
THE WORST ROAD IN AMERICA

Germantown Avenue was such a treacherous sea of mud and ooze during the Colonial period that horses and carriages were alleged to have disappeared forever

*America's oldest funeral home, Kirk & Nice
on historic Germantown Avenue.*

into the slime. It was characterized as "the worst road in America" until it was paved and improved as a toll road in 1800.

It's no speedway today with its trolley tracks and stretches of bone-shaking cobblestone. But there may be no other street in America so rich in history. Virtually every stone house, church, graveyard and business along its length has some historic significance. One old Germantown guidebook is simply an address-by-address stroll up the avenue. This chapter takes a look at two of Germantown Avenue's interesting, and of course old, businesses.

KIRK & NICE

It's worth visiting America's oldest funeral home before one becomes the horizontal guest of honor because it's truly an interesting place and not at all depressing. In fact, it's a real friendly place.

The present head of the family-owned firm is Mariann Henderson, a surprisingly jolly undertaker who would like to make her own exit with a gala New Orleans-style jazz funeral and ponders throwing a Halloween open-house for kids.

The business dates to 1761 when Jacob Knorr opened a carpenter's shop that made furniture and developed a nice sideline in coffins. In those days there were no funeral homes.

On Oct. 4, 1777, the hottest fighting in the Battle of Germantown took place practically in front of Knorr's shop. A Kirk & Nice pamphlet says, ". . . more coffins were made that day than any day before or after."

In the 19th century the shop was taken over by John Nice and his sons. Soon apprentice B. Frank Kirk became a partner. A Knorr got back into the business at some point. So, it's been all Knorrs, Kirks and Nices for 230 years. Henderson's late husband, John R. Henderson, was a Kirk.

The business has always

An old grandfather clock made in Germantown, of course.

been at the same location, although the current sprawling structure dates only to the 1930s. Kirk & Nice holds a special place in the hearts of Germantowners, a subspecies of *homo Philadelphius* that really knows how to cling to traditions. The funeral home has buried them all: patrician and common folk, black and white, Catholic, Protestant, Jew – even a Buddhist or two.

A lot of interesting artifacts have accumulated since 1761. And there seems to be an odd tradition among Germantowners of willing objects to Kirk & Nice. As a result, the funeral home has a large collection of interesting and historic objects that give a museumlike feel to the place. Its halls are lined with display cases, its walls festooned with old paintings and prints. Its huge lounge is a wonderful Victorian parlor filled with intriguing curios, several old grandfather's clocks, a huge oriental rug and lots of vintage furniture.

It's quite an eclectic collection. One case displays German Bibles and prayer books, the work of Germantown's own Christopher Saur, who printed America's first Bibles in a European language in 1743. The Bibles are next to a tall case filled with hundreds of toy sol-

diers. Still another case shows off colored glass items, paperweights and Toby jugs.

The wall art is mainly scenes of Old Philadelphia and Germantown, but there's also a painting of a Pueblo Indian, for no particular reason. One item bequeathed to Kirk & Nice is a portrait of Lafayette painted while he was a guest in Germantown. It was the possession of one family for generations until it was willed to Kirk & Nice. Another item left to the funeral home by a wood-carving clergyman, is a representation of the "40-mule team" of Borax soap fame. A table in the lounge holds two very old and interesting Victrolas. Old photo albums on the table are filled with typical family snapshots dating from the 1920s. They are Henderson family albums. The owner figured why let them lie around at home and gather dust?

The funeral home has many vintage bills and receipts for caskets, ice, hearse rental and such, some dating to the 18th century. A bill dated 1798 for a walnut coffin is in pounds and shillings.

A few steps up Germantown Avenue from the funeral home are two historic treasures worth seeing: the one-room Concord School House built in 1775, and the adjacent Upper Germantown Burial Ground, dedicated in 1692.

About 25 Revolutionary War soldiers are buried in the old cemetery – not to mention veterans of the War of 1812. The old schoolhouse has been fixed up as a museum, but it's locked and opened only by appointment.

Kirk & Nice is located at the intersection of Germantown Avenue and Washington Lane. Call for an appointment. Phone: 438-6328

The spacious Kirk & Nice lounge has a museumlike quality.

A painting of a scene on Germantown Avenue is one of the many gifts now hanging on the walls of Kirk & Nice.

CUNNINGHAM PIANO

As Germantown institutions go, this is a mere babe in swaddling clothes, founded only a century ago in 1891 in Center City, moving up to Germantown in the 1920s.

Still, there is history attached to this address: Author Louisa May Alcott was born on the very spot in 1832. The family moved when she was

Display cases filled with interesting objects line the walls at Kirk & Nice.

only 2. Want more history? Chubby Checker bought a piano here. So have concert pianists and many local concert halls and theaters.

But you don't go to Cunningham Piano for history. You go to see pianos being rebuilt, revitalized, reborn, through the slow, patient skills of handcraftsmen. The company specializes in rebuilding old pianos and happily provides free tours of its piano workshop lasting about 40 minutes.

Here are skills rarely seen anymore, skills that can be learned only through a long apprenticeship. In some cases it takes months to rebuild and refinish a piano, but many believe an old piano from a prestige company is superior to just about anything new. A handsome rebuilt Steinway in the showroom carries a price tag of $52,000. In fact, the company will only invest the time and effort of rebuilding into a really fine piano.

The factory is in an old brick building just around the corner from the showroom on Germantown Avenue. Each technician and refinisher works alone. As much work goes into hand-rubbing and polishing the wood as in replacing strings and sounding boards.

In its early years the company manufactured new pianos and player pianos. During the Depression, founder Patrick Cunningham sold the company to the late Louis Cohen, whose two daughters now run the business.

Cohen had a particularly impoverished childhood, starting as a struggling piano tuner going door-to-door in search of work. His daughters say he had a deep admiration and interest in Abraham Lincoln, who also overcame an impoverished childhood. Cohen became a passionate collector of Lincoln memorabilia, which explains why the walls of the piano company are covered with pictures and items related to Honest Abe.

Cunningham Piano is at 5427 Germantown Avenue. Call for tour information. Phone: 438-3200.

* * * * *

An expert Cunningham technician brings a vintage piano back to life.

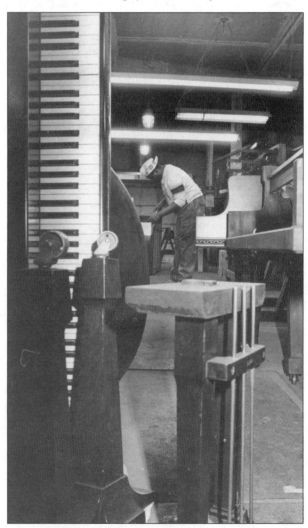
Meticulous handwork characterizes the work at the Cunningham Piano Company.

Chapter 6

BUCKS COUNTY'S
MASTER CASTLE BUILDER
The Mercer Mile

He was an eccentric genius, an American original. And during his varied life Henry Chapman Mercer (1856–1930) created the most unique, imaginative, whimsical, oddly fascinating structures in the Delaware Valley.

The three concrete "castles" that make up "the Mercer Mile" are arguably this region's most appealing attractions. A visitor to the Philadelphia area with time to see only one sight can skip Independence Hall: it looks exactly like the pictures in the history books.

Instead, take the 30-mile ride through bucolic Bucks County to Doylestown and sign up for the 90-minute tour of Henry Mercer's wonderfully weird home, Fonthill. Time permitting, see the nearby Mercer Museum. Finally, take the self-guided tour of Mercer's Moravian Pottery & Tile Works.

Mercer was a Doylestown native of inherited wealth, a Harvard graduate, a pioneering archaeologist/anthropologist and the craftsman/businessman who created the still-admired Moravian ceramic tiles.

He was also a cantankerous eccentric with a scholar's intellect and the unfettered imagination of an adolescent dreamer. Mercer kicked off his career with meticulous digging and studying of prehistoric sites in North and Central America.

But in the late 1890s, Mercer threw himself into a new quest, which must have made scholars snicker and his neighbors feel he had graduated from oddball into a full-blown crackpot junk collector. He turned his back on ancient history and began the passionate collecting of tools and common artifacts of the recent American past.

Industrialization was rapidly replacing handcrafts, old arts and skills. Mercer started buying – or rescuing from trash heaps – every old tool, household item and farming implement he could find. He called it "archaeology turned upside down."

This, somehow, led to a fascination with the craft of making decorative tiles by old hand techniques and the establishment of his own business. Mercer's Moravian tiles were soon in demand for expensive mansions and by builders who wanted some distinctive, artsy touches. His tile mosaics can be found in the Rockefeller estate, the chapel at West Point, the Pennsylvania Capitol and many grand hotels.

But it is Henry Mercer as builder, that interests us here. As a youth he had traveled in Europe and become enraptured by old castles. In 1907, Mercer began building his dream castle on 70 acres of Doylestown farmland – without detailed plans, without an architect.

He was a fan of the relatively new poured-concrete method of construction. With the aid of a few workmen, Mercer completed his castle in four years. In the process, he invented new building techniques for poured-concrete structures: He built from the inside out, designing as he progressed. He incorporated an existing farmhouse by pouring concrete over it.

Every room is different in shape, size, style. It seems that no two windows are exactly the same. He often fashioned built-in furniture of concrete, such as chests of drawers and vanity tables.

The house is a maze. It's filled with twisting stairways, hidden stairways, odd alcoves, vaulted ceilings. The exact number of rooms is a matter of debate.

There are hundreds of whimsical or inventive touches: footprints of Mercer's huge dog in a cement staircase, Babylonian cuneiform tablets used as wall decoration, the impressions of old stove-plates decorating a ceiling. And in every room are Mercer's famous tiles, adding color and beauty to fireplaces, floors or ceilings.

There is really nothing comparable to Fonthill. A world traveler from New Zealand said he'd been more impressed by a huge estate in California. "But this is totally unique."

Mercer went on to build a new tile works and a museum to display the thousands of items in his collection. Both buildings are as singular and as wildly imaginative as Fonthill.

The Mercer Museum is like no other museum. Even those with no interest in the items will be captivated by the structure and the layout of the place. Again, it's a sort of castle, built from the inside out in solid cement. The interior contains seven tiers of galleries and a central court. There are no traditional museum display cases.

Instead, there are scores of cells (they look like jail cells) each containing the tools and artifacts of a particular craftsman: clockmaker, hatter, cigar maker, confectioner, butcher, salt maker, carpenter, etc. There are good written

COURTESY OF MERCER MUSEUM

The design of the building and the display system make the Mercer Museum unique.

Fonthill, a whimsical concrete maze, was Henry Mercer's dream castle.

At Fonthill fireplaces can be anywhere and staircases sometimes go nowhere.

explanations of most items and processes. It's impossible not to learn something new and interesting.

One fascinating aspect of the place, is all the huge objects suspended or protruding from all levels in the central court. Fire engines, wagons, a whaleboat (filled with tools of the trade), plows – all just hang there. The growing collection numbers 40,000 objects, some rather surprising, such as the complete gallows and scaffold that once stretched necks at Bucks County Prison.

Henry Ford once declared it the only museum he was sufficiently interested in visiting.

The Moravian Tile Works, next to Fonthill, is also a tourist attraction featuring working artisans who create tiles from the original Mercer designs. The building is a fantasy in concrete with the look of a Spanish monastery. But only a small portion of the rambling plant is open. A museum shop sells the handmade, handpainted tiles.

All three attractions are open seven days a week, except major holidays. It is wise to call ahead and reserve a place on the Fonthill tours. All three buildings have an admission charge. Phone: 348-9461

✳ ✳ ✳ ✳ ✳

Chapter 7

THE FAITHFUL FRIENDS
OF FREDDIE COCOZZA
Mario Lanza Museum

If all the entertainers who were born and bred in the rowhouses of South Philadelphia were stacked one on top of the other, it would be a more ridiculous sight than the city's Clothes Pin statue and a lot higher, too.

There were Joey Bishop, Chubby Checker, James Darren, Buddy Greco, Frankie Avalon, Marian Anderson and Eddie Fisher, to name a a handful. But none created the excitement nor attained the adulation in the old neighborhood to match Freddie Cocozza.

Freddie adopted his mother's maiden name and as Mario Lanza became an "International Star," a bona fide "Hollywood Star." And just about every Italian-American in South Philly proudly basked in the reflected glory of his fame and celebrity. And when he died at age 38 in Rome, an entire neighborhood went into shocked mourning.

MARILYN A. SHAPIRO

A prized bust of Mario Lanza.

"There was a viewing at Leonetti's Funeral Home on Broad Street," recalls Mary Papola. "People stood in a line outside for hours to get in. Once you got inside, you stopped for two seconds at the coffin and had to move on. I remember, he was so heavy, he hardly fit into the coffin. . . . Then his wife took the body to Hollywood where there was another funeral and he was buried.

"See over there? That was the crucifix that was on the coffin. These were the mass cards," explains the executive secretary of the Mario Lanza Institute pointing out two historic artifacts among hundreds on display in the Mario Lanza Museum.

Yes, Philadelphia has a Mario Lanza Institute, and a Mario Lanza Museum and a Mario Lanza Park. And in Southwest Philadelphia there is a Mario Lanza Boulevard.

The Museum is a large room on the third floor of the venerable Settlement Music School, where Lanza took his first singing lessons. It's chock-full of rare Mario memorabilia.

Paintings, sketches, photographs and sculptures of the singer line the walls. There are framed photocopies of Freddie's birth certificate and death certificate. Visitors can view his identification bracelet and his 1935 Vare Junior High School class photo.

There's a framed dollar bill with Mario's face where George Washington's mug should be. There are various congratulatory telegrams sent to the singer and a letter from Harry Truman thanking Mario for a record.

There are news clippings, movie posters, gold records, notes and letters written by this famous son of South Philly. There are also commemorative cups, plates and vases bearing his handsome likeness.

Hanging on a clothes rack are a shirt and sweater once worn by the star. Inside a glass case is a tentlike tuxedo jacket that would be baggy on Pavarotti. The average-size sweater and shirt and the wide jacket illustrate Lanza's yo-yoing weight problem.

Apparently the singer's body could no longer take the overeating and drug-aided weight loss regime. His heart gave out in an Italian clinic in 1959. His wife committed suicide five months after the tenor's death. His mother, who had been a seamstress at South Philadelphia's Defense Department Support Center, took over the rearing of the couple's four children in California.

With the encouragement of his mother, loyal fans in the old neighborhood formed the Mario Lanza Institute. The organization sponsors an annual voice competition and awards scholarship funds to the winners.

The money is raised by an annual Mario Lanza Day Ball at Palumbo's Restaurant early each October. The day begins with services in the church where Lanza once sang "Ave Maria." It's followed by a reception in the house on Chris-

MARILYN A. SHAPIRO

Among the items of Mario memorabilia is a tent-sized jacket illustrating the singer's weight problem.

tian Street near 6th where Lanza was born and which is now occupied by two of Lanza's aunts.

The evening Ball attracts about 400 people, and usually a handful fly in from Great Britain for the affair. Yes, there is a British Mario Lanza Society numbering nearly 400 faithful. It has its own annual ball and prizes for young singers. Occasionally other European fans make a pilgrimage to the museum, sometimes spending several days wallowing in Lanza lore.

The museum was an outgrowth of the Institute founded in 1976. The collection's first home was the back room of Nick Petrella's record store on Snyder Avenue. Most of the items came from Lanza's estate through his mother.

Petrella, now retired, is like most of the dozen or so hardcore South Philly Lanza addicts whose labors keep the ball and the museum going – he barely knew Freddie Cocozza.

"My first music store was near 20th and Mercy where his parents lived," explains Petrella. "His

Museum curator Joseph Siciliano was an old pal of Lanza.

father would come into the store and tell about his son and how he was going to be a big star. . . . His first movie, "That Midnight Kiss," came out in 1948. There had been a lot of local publicity about it. There was a three-record sound track. It was his first record, and I bought 4,000.

"He came to Philly when the movie was released. There was a big parade. The streets were decorated. I was the only store with his record. In one day, I sold 3,800 records at $1 each. Can you imagine taking in $3,800 in one day?" smiles Petrella. "This was 1948. I usually took in, maybe $40, $50, during a whole day. I'll never forget it."

Lanza made only seven films. "The Great Caruso" in 1951 was probably his best. His records sold well and have been reissued on tape and compact disc. But his experience in legitimate opera was minimal. Most opera aficionados pooh-poohed Mario as a serious singer. He was driven to prove himself and moved to Rome with plans of conquering the world of real opera, and died there.

You'll never convince those who keep the museum alive that Lanza isn't the greatest singer of our age. They have produced a video tape to be played for museum visitors. Narrator Joe Curreri, who remembers playing football

The entrance to the Mario Lanza Museum inside the Settlement Music School.

with Lanza in his youth, proclaims Lanza's voice "unmatched by any other singer in our lifetime . . . Arturo Toscanini said it all: 'The greatest voice in the 20th century' . . . Mario Lanza touched us all."

It's fun to visit the museum and meet his die-hard fans. Just about all are collecting Social Security checks. They wonder and worry: Will a new generation emerge to keep the flame burning?

The Mario Lanza Museum, third floor, Settlement School of Music, 416 Queen Street. Open 10 a.m. to 3:30 p.m. Monday through Saturday. Closed Saturdays in July and August. Phone: 468-3623

* * * * *

Mounted, painted and live, Mill Grove is full of birds.

Chapter 8

THE BIRDMAN OF THE PERKIOMEN

Mill Grove

Anyone who has ever driven the Schuylkill Expressway to the Valley Forge Exit of the Pennsylvania Turnpike is familiar with a nightmarish tangle of highways and jug handles accompanied by a muddle of confusing signs.

Undaunted by this nerve-wracking asphalt maze, visitors from as far away as California and Canada manage, somehow, to find Mill Grove, the first American home of naturalist John James Audubon. Their daring and determination is rewarded with a tranquilizing hour or two spent roaming one of the most scenic, pleasantly bucolic spots in the Delaware Valley.

The handsome Colonial-era home and outbuildings sit on 170 acres of woods, fields and manicured lawn on high bluffs overlooking a particularly unspoiled stretch of Perkiomen Creek. Hiking trails on the estate follow the creek through untouched woodlands. Since the place is rarely crowded, Mill Grove is an ideal destination for young lovers. It's also highly recommended for nature lovers, lovers of early American architecture and lovers of a cheap place to take the family; it's free.

Bird lovers, of course, already know about Mill Grove. Those who have read any of the numerous biographies of the French-born artist–naturalist, know that Audubon lived at Mill Grove for only three years. But they were the most idyllic and relaxed in his life. It was here he found a wife and his passion for painting birds.

In the 1980 book "On the Road with John James Audubon" by Mary Durant and Michael Harwood, the first chapter focuses on Mill Grove. The book's first words quote Audubon: "In Pennsylvania, a beautiful state . . . my father gave me what Americans call a beautiful plantation, refreshed during the summer's heat by the waters of the Schuylkill River and transversed by a creek named Perkioming. Its fine woodlands, its extensive acres, its fields crowned with evergreens, offer many subjects for my pencil. It was there that I commenced my simple and agreeable studies, with as little concern about the future as if the world were made for me."

Enjoying the green vista from the porch of Mill Grove.

The ivy-covered stone house dates to 1762 and was purchased as an American investment by the senior Audubon in 1789. Young Audubon arrived in 1804, a carefree, handsome 18-year-old. While a tenant farmer worked the land, the Frenchman spent his time wandering about, trapping, hunting, painting and impressing the locals with his marvelous ice skating talent. Skating on the creek nearly cost his life when he fell into a air-hole but was lucky enough to pop out of another hole some 40 feet downstream.

It's still an idyllic, unspoiled spot that has not changed much since Audubon's day. Ed Graham, the cordial, longtime curator says 180 species of birds have been seen on the property, drawn, perhaps, by the many huge, old shade trees.

The three-story house has been turned into a museum with 11 rooms open to the public. They are filled with original bird and animal paintings by Audubon, stuffed birds, birds' eggs and educational displays.

Audubon's greatest work is the large-sheet, four-volume "Birds of North America." Only 190 sets were printed. Each set has 435 prints; and each print was separately hand-painted. The engraving and painting work went on from 1826 to 1838. The cost of each set was $1,000, a high-ticket item today and a huge outlay in the early 1800s.

The fact that Audubon found 190 people willing to pay such an enormous sum says a lot about his talent. About 100 sets are still intact and a complete original set is worth more than $3 million. Mill Grove has a complete set of

More mounted birds and memorabilia in the attic of Mill Grove.

what is often called "the double-elephants folio," and many single prints hang on its walls. "Double-elephant" was a paper size – the largest available at the time. Audubon painted each bird to actual size, including eagles, swans and hawks.

One surprising aspect of Mill Grove is that the estate once contained both a lead and a copper mine. Philadelphia paint maker Samuel Wetherill purchased Mill Grove in 1813 as a source of lead for Wetherill Paint. The property stayed in the family until 1951 when it was sold to Montgomery County. The 160-foot-deep copper mine employed 200 miners at its peak in the 1850s. During World War II federal geologists came out to examine the copper mine but decided against reopening it.

A scenic tree-lined drive leads to the Audubon house, Mill Grove.

Mill Grove is open Tuesday through Sunday, 10 a.m. to 4 p.m. Follow the Schuylkill Expressway to Exit 202 South/422-West. Follow Route 422. Take the first exit after crossing Betzwood Bridge, 363 North/Audubon. Make left at first traffic light, Audubon Road. Follow Audubon Road to its end. Phone: 666-5593.

✳ ✳ ✳ ✳ ✳

Colonial-era houses frame the shady courtyard at Workman's Place in Southwark.

Chapter 9

YE AUTHENTIC OLDE PHILADELPHIA

Workman's Place

There's something about Society Hill that's just a bit too neat and handsome. There's something about Elfreth's Alley that's a bit unreal and museumlike.

But there's something about Workman's Place – the look, the feel, the texture – that's real and provides a pretty authentic glimpse of early Philadelphia.

Not surprisingly, you'll find this courtyard cluster of 18th and 19th century homes in the oldest neighborhood in the city – an area well settled by Swedes and English even before William Penn sailed up the Delaware. For nearly three centuries the neighborhood was called Southwark. A couple of decades ago some clever real estate promoters decided to yuppie-up the blue collar image with a new name: Queen Village.

Workman's Place may possibly be America's oldest existing rental housing for workmen, but that's not how it got its name. Another name for the complex is Mifflin Court. In 1748 George Mifflin (his son, Thomas, became Pennsylvania's first governor) built several small brick houses to rent to local waterfront workers.

In 1812, a lumber merchant named John Workman purchased several lots from the Mifflin family and erected three-and-a-half-story apartment-type houses in front of the older houses.

The 1748 Mifflin houses and the 1812 Workman houses form a sort of quadrangle around a spacious courtyard, which gives Mifflin Court/Workman's Place a third name. Longtime residents and neighbors all call it "The Big Yard."

From the beginning the people of Workman's Place and Southwark were mostly callused-handed riverfront workers, stevedores and bargemen. In the early years of this century Polish immigrants settled in the old neighborhood and took over many of the riverfront jobs.

Today Southwark may be old and quaint, but in the early decades of this century it was simply an overcrowded slum. In 1906 Lydia S. Clark, a landlord with a highly developed social consciousness, purchased Workman's Place and hired the reformist Octavia Hill Society to manage the 36-unit complex.

A gate opens to the courtyard at Workman's Place near Front and Pemberton.

The organization was founded in 1896 by progressive thinkers to provide the poor with decent housing. In 1942 Octavia Hill purchased Workman's Place and still owns it.

A settlement house was set up in one unit, and among its more important functions was providing hot showers for two cents. It wasn't until 1951 that indoor plumbing was installed at Workman's Place. A couple of residents still remember using outhouses in the courtyard and the good works of Mrs. Mott's settlement house.

Rents are still relatively low and some tenants are still blue collar folk. Just a few blocks north is chic, hip South Street, but here at Workman's Place there is still a feeling of old Southwark.

And there's the feeling of Colonial Philadelphia. One of the Mifflin houses on Pemberton Street still has the date "1748" visible in the brickwork, and a neighboring house sports the initials "G.M." for George Mifflin.

Those Mifflin houses, facing the big courtyard with its large shade trees, are as cozy and quaint as any in the city. One neighborhood couple that moved into a 1748 trinity more than 25 years ago has become affluent enough to live almost anywhere. But they've become so attached to the quiet colonial coziness that leaving, they say, is unthinkable.

For those not familiar with the charms of Queen Village, Workman's Place makes a good starting point for an informal walking tour of the neighborhood. The neighborhood is one of America's great reservoirs of 18th century housing. There are scores of modest homes built in the 1700s on streets too narrow for automobiles.

Many lovers of historic houses still rage and fume over the horrendous losses caused by the

A cozy 18th century "trinity house" with a reasonable rent.

*Looking out the parlor window of a home
built nearly 250 years ago.*

A patriotic window display.

construction of Route I-95 in the 1960s. In fact, some 17th century structures were bulldozed into kindling to make way for the interstate.

Still, there's a lot worth seeing on Queen, Kenilworth, Hancock (a fabulous street), Catharine, Fitzwater, Monroe and narrow Kauffman streets. Visit Old Swedes' Church and the Sparks Shot Tower. On many blocks clapboard houses have miraculously survived more than 200 years of habitation and fire hazards.

The survival of so much old housing in more or less original condition is explained by the fact that Southwark was always a neighborhood of workers and artisans of modest means. They kept their property in repair, but few had the money to really "modernize."

Workman's Place is located on Front Street between Pemberton and Fitzwater with a courtyard in the rear.

✳ ✳ ✳ ✳ ✳

47

There are no straight lines in Wharton Esherick's studio; even the roof seems to sag.

Chapter 10

THE TWISTED WORLD OF ESHERICK
Wharton Esherick Studio

Neither words nor photographs can adequately portray the weird, wonderful world created by artist Wharton Esherick on a wooded hillside not far from Valley Forge.

This one you have to see for yourself.

Everything about the studio/residence created by the avante garde woodworker during 40 years is totally different, eccentric and wildly imaginative – from his unconventional toilet seat to the real mastodon tusk that forms a handrail on his one of a kind double-spiral stairway.

Art mavens are probably already familiar with Esherick. His wood sculptures can be seen at the Smithsonian, the Metropolitan Museum of Art and the Philadelphia Art Museum.

Born in Philadelphia in 1887, Esherick moved to an old Chester County farmhouse in 1913 to paint, but soon evolved into a master woodcarver and furniture maker. Clients were captivated by his unusual picture frames and then went gaga over the furniture they saw in his studio.

Esherick said there were no straight lines in nature. And there are certainly no straight lines in his artwork or his studio. The studio, which first appeared as a modernistic stone farmhouse in 1926, is full of curves. The roof curves like a swayback mule. The walls curve to simulate the way a tree curves as it grows from the ground.

The studio grew over 40 years without any formal plan or blueprints. He added a two-story, wood-plank addition in 1930. Later he appended a rounded concrete tower, dubbed "The Silo" to an already strange building.

An old friend of the artist, now in her 90s, lives on the upper floor of the silo portion. A few yards from this original studio is an even wilder creation, Esherick's second studio built in 1956 when he needed additional work space. The design was provided by famed architect and friend Louis Kahn. The Kahn building is basically three connected concrete hexagons. This building is now the residence of Esherick's daughter, Ruth Bascom, and her husband and is not part of the public tour. If the outside is any indication, the interior must be fascinating.

Esherick also built a garage of wood planks which seems to defy all laws of wood and geometry. The roof is totally crooked, the walls asymmetrical: one wall convex, the opposite concave.

The orginal workshop became the artist's display area. Since many of his sculpture pieces were carved from tall logs, extra height was required. So he dug a deep pit in the floor, called the "sculpture well." Several of his soaring, museum-quality carvings are on display.

Visitors get a guided tour of the studio which lasts 60 to 90 minutes. It's not a particularly large space, yet it's hardly enough time to take in all the unique details and objet d'art. Some visitors return again and again.

Even a pull-chain on a lamp operates differently than other pull-chains and has a piece of interesting sculpture as a pull tab. The rain gutter on the roof is a wonderful piece of sculptured wood, so are the hand-carved door latches.

His porcelain toilet is plum in color. The sink is made of copper and has an odd shape. The kitchen sink also has an unusual shape. There's a kitchen cutting board shaped to fit the sink which ingeniously adds counter space.

Esherick once picked up a barrel of long hammer handles at a sale with no particular use in mind. When friends at the Hedgerow Theater asked him to make chairs for the rehearsal hall, the ever-creative Esherick devised the world's first hammer-handle chair. He also created chairs from surplus wagon wheels. He hated handles and devised simple and unusual ways for opening drawers in desks and chests.

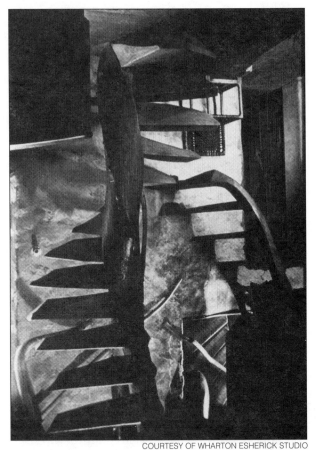

COURTESY OF WHARTON ESHERICK STUDIO

The famous twin spiral-stairway at the Esherick studio uses a real mastodon tusk as a handrail.

The twin spiral studio-stairway is one of his most famous pieces. A friend mining in the West discovered a twisted, six-foot-long mastodon tusk and knew Esherick would find a use for it.

Esherick appears to have been an independent and slightly reclusive character who could be quite ornery. If he didn't like a person, he wouldn't take a commission from him. Clients never knew what he would produce, what the price would be, nor when he would finish the job. And the last thing you'd want to do was to pressure or nag the artist to complete a commission. He didn't like visitors in his studio, not even his own children.

His friends included the writers Theodore Dreiser and Sherwood Anderson. He designed the tombstone for Anderson's grave. Of course it is gracefully curved.

His children established his original studio as a museum, leaving it exactly as it was when he died. His clothes are still in his bedroom drawers.

Directions to Wharton Esherick Studio can best be obtained by calling 644-5822. Guided tours are provided only on Saturdays and Sundays from March through December.

✳ ✳ ✳ ✳ ✳

Everything, including the chess set, in artist Wharton Esherick's bedroom is unique.

Old-fashioned fun at Smith Memorial Playground.

Chapter 11

DELIGHTS OF A
HISTORIC SLIDING BOARD
Smith Memorial Playground

How much can a person approaching 50 remember about fifth grade? Not much, but I can certainly remember my fifth-grade class trip to Smith Playground. I still remember the excitement and anticipation leading up to the big day. And of course I remember the Giant Slide.

The trip to Smith Memorial Playground in Fairmount Park might well be the most commonly shared childhood memory of all Philadelphians of every age, every social class, every neighborhood.

By official estimate more than nine million kids have romped and rolled in Smith Playground since its opening in 1899. Ask any native if he remembers Smith Playground and the odds are 3-to-1 on an affirmative reply.

It's still there just off 33rd Street in the park, a place amazingly untouched by time. More amazing, in an age of Disney World and electronic space games, this hoary, antique of a playground still delights and excites the peanut gallery.

Its six fenced acres are filled with sturdy old-fashioned playground equipment, picnic tables and a large, mansionlike building for kids under five called the Playhouse.

The Playground's most beloved and famous attraction is a wide wooden sliding board constructed in 1908. Roofed and enclosed by walls on three sides, it is what everyone remembers: the famed Giant Slide! It's still the first place the kids run. Some have been known to slide for hours. Several kids abreast can slither down its 12-foot width, creating all sorts of possibilities for bumping and entanglement.

Smith Playground is in Fairmount Park but independently funded and administered. It was a gift to the children of the city from Richard Smith (1821-1894) in memory of his only son, Stanford Smith. It would be logical to asssume that Stanford died in childhood. In fact, the lad was 40 when he passed on.

Smith was a wealthy manufacturer of printing type and lived his later years in Paris. His will provided for the playground and for a monument to the Civil War dead. The monument was built in front of Memorial Hall in West Fairmount Park and includes a statue of

Smith, himself, along with several famous military heroes.

Smith Playground is still supported by the endowment left by the philanthropist. In the 1920s, three other playgrounds were built in poor neighborhoods with excess funds from the Smith estate. More than simple playgrounds, the new facilities also provided teen clubs, organized activities and professional social workers. Apparently the Depression depleted the kitty and the other sites were closed.

One interesting aspect of Smith's will was a provision that boys over 10 years old be barred from the Playground. The exclusionary rule has since been raised to 12 to accommo-date the many school groups that visit the playground. The stricture probably grew out of a desire to create a safe haven for little shavers free of big kids, who might bully and usurp playthings.

In the Playhouse, the rule is only those five or younger and no parents admitted. It's a wonderful place with a lot of old-fashioned stuff that should stir nostalgic childhood memories.

There are little tables for tea parties, a play stove for baking pretend cakes. The most fun can be found in a room called "Smithville," where toddlers climb into old-fashioned pedal cars and drive down painted streets. The make-

Muscle-power provides the motion on this merry-go-round.

The playhouse at Smith Playground is filled with toys for toddlers.

believe village has a working traffic light, miniature gas pumps and scaled down parking meters that work – on pennies.

Another Playhouse room, designated The Pieces Playroom, contains car tires and various over-sized building block-style squares and ovals for creative construction. Still another room has a great big, sturdy, old-fashioned dollhouse.

If you think today's tots are too sophisticated for sturdy, simple toys and make-believe, watch a tiny motorist cruise Smithville, making appropriate motor and honking noises, totally absorbed in highway "driving."

During the school year, the place attracts busloads of school groups, as many as 1,000 kids a day. Summer days and Saturdays may be quieter.

Smith Playground is located behind the golf driving range at 33rd and Oxford in the Strawberry Mansion section of Fairmount Park. Hours are Monday through Saturday, 9 a.m. to 4:45 p.m.

✳ ✳ ✳ ✳ ✳

The Giant Slide has been a Smith Playground favorite since 1908.

*The dining room at the Adriatic Club
is filled on weekends.*

Chapter 12

FROM ALBANIANS TO ZAMBIANS,
A CLUB FOR EVERY ETHNIC

Philadelphia is a smorgasbord of ethnicity. Each group has its neighborhood strongholds, social clubs, benevolent societies, credit unions. Older immigrant societies and clubs – Irish, German, Jewish, Polish, Italian – manage to hold on despite aging and shrinking membership lists. Recent arrivals build vibrant new associations. There are a host of new Haitian, Hispanic and Asian organizations. This chapter focuses on two vintage ethnic clubs.

The German Society of Pennsylvania on Spring Garden Street dates to 1888.

AUSTRIAN SEACOAST BENEVOLENT SOCIETY

The name should perplex anyone with even rudimentary knowledge of world geography. As we all know, Austria, in the heart of Central Europe, has no seacoast. But when this immigrant society was founded in 1890, the sprawling Austrian Empire did, indeed, have a coastline. Today it's part of Yugoslavia. In fact, the Seacoasters' club is better known in the neighborhood as "the Adriatic Club."

There was plenty of work for a maritime people in lower Port Richmond at the turn of the century. The neighborhood had large shipyards and a busy waterfront. Reading Railroad coal barges by the score were loaded here and towed to Atlantic ports.

A strong Croatian-speaking community settled near the docks. They established several organizations: the Croatian Fraternal Union, the Croatian Singing Society, but only the Seacoasters remain.

The organization met at several locations before settling into a cozy former Protestant church built in 1842. The society's charter, written in both Croatian and English, now hangs in the club's office, stating the organization's purposes as providing health and burial insurance.

That function has never changed. Neither has the cost of the insurance: $1.25 to $2.75 a month. The maximum death benefit is $900. In cases of serious illness, the insured can collect $14 a week for a period of 13 weeks. And there's even enough money left over for tiny scholarship grants for the members' kids.

Of course, it's not the benefits that keeps the society alive. Despite its shrinking membership the place is far from deserted, thanks to the large number of "social" members who use the place as an after-hours drinking and dancing spot on weekends.

Except for a wall mural depicting the port area of Dubrovnik, the bar and dining areas are of little interest. But upstairs are two ancient bowling lanes that might be the oldest in the city. Down in the basement are bocce courts that haven't been used in 40 years.

The well-worn bowling lanes will bring nostalgic smiles to those old enough to remember nimble, hard-working "pinboys." Here human pinsetters still perch on a ledge to avoid being mangled by oncoming balls and hop down to set the pins and manually return the ball.

The bocce courts were built at a great expense that included importing surface clay from Italy. There was great Italian influence and mingling of peoples along the Adriatic Coast. Many of the immigrants spoke both Italian and Croatian and the club's kitchen was once famous for gnocci, bacalao and calamari.

Not much remains of the old Croatian community. There are about 50 society members: the sons and grandsons of the immigrants including a retired sea captain who makes wonderful model ships, an old tugboat hand who tells corny jokes, and other former waterfront types. There's still a ladies' auxiliary and a tiny youth group. About 150 people celebrated the society's centennial in 1990. But the days are long gone when the ability to speak Croatian was a requirement to sit on the Austrian Seacoast Society board of directors.

The Austrian Seacoast Society/Adriatic Club is located at 2644 E. Huntingdon Street.

GERMAN SOCIETY OF PENNSYLVANIA

Like the Wagner Institute, this is another building that remains wonderfully frozen in time. Those with an overwhelming urge to escape to the grace and tranquillity of the 19th century will love the place.

Founded in 1764, the society holds the distinction of being the oldest German organization in America. It also bills itself as the first American immigrant-aid-group of any kind.

German history in America begins in 1683 with the arrival of the 13 founding families of Germantown. The society was founded to aid fellow German immigrants, particularly exploited indentured servants. By the time it built its present quarters in 1888, the society's principal role was supporting and maintaining German culture.

It's a large, handsome building filled with fine woodwork, plaster work, antiques, memorabilia and objet d'art. The auditorium used for lectures and concerts looks as if Jenny Lind was the last performer to cross its stage. The basement is a rathskeller used for parties and luncheons and seems more modern than the rest of the building.

The society's major boast is the handsome, sedate and timeless old library. Outside of a few major universities, it houses the largest collection of German reading material in America. The age and rarity of the collection makes the library a unique resource.

The classic library at the German Society of Pennsylvania.

German scholars have come to Philadelphia to search its bookcases for material that can no longer be found in Deutschland, and it's a primary source for anyone studying German immigration and German-American culture.

Pennsylvania had the largest German community in early America, so books, daily newspapers, pamphlets, state ordinances, even farmer's almanacs, were printed in German. Benjamin Franklin published works in German, and the first Bibles in any European language printed in America were the work of Christopher Saur of Germantown.

The 45,000 book collection includes many of these rare early works, but it is strongest in the popular reading of the 19th century. The collection was seen primarily as a "volksbibliothek," or people's library, emphasizing popular history, travel books and novels.

Members like to tell the story of a University of Pennsylvania student who traveled to Germany to gather material for a doctoral dissertation on the 19th century German novel, but failed to locate several key books. She found the missing tomes, of course at the German Society. Considering that the society has never spent money on preservation or modern climate controls, the books are in surprisingly good shape.

On display in the building are many museum-quality items relating to German-Americans in Philadelphia: banners, photos, paintings, documents, sculpture.

The most colorful corner of the building is the clubroom of the local chapter of an international German-speaking fraternity known as "Schlaraffia." Members spoof chivalry and knighthood by assuming silly names and costumes and by "dueling" in German verse or prose. Its meeting room is cluttered with the outlandish fraternal paraphernalia including dueling swords, beer steins, humorous coats-of-arms and caricatures.

The German Society of Pennsylvania is located at 7th and Spring Garden. Call regarding library hours and social functions. Phone: 627-4365.

✳ ✳ ✳ ✳ ✳

Playing cards found on a Civil War battlefield.

Chapter 13

JOHNNY CAME MARCHING HOME WITH SOUVENIRS

Even before the gunsmoke cleared from the battlefields, survivors were prowling the blood-soaked ground collecting souvenirs. Those who lived through it were well aware of the monumental importance and unprecedented drama of the Civil War. Mementos were eagerly sought and saved.

When the bloodshed ended, veterans' organizations were founded and the post-homes often became the repositories of war souvenirs and documents. This is how Philadelphia became home to two of the finest Civil War museums in the nation. Until very recently both operated as private preserves of the veterans' descendants. Today both seek visitors, and Civil War buffs travel great distances to marvel at treasures most Philadelphians don't know exist.

CIVIL WAR MUSEUM & LIBRARY

Among those with war mementos in abundance were the members of the Military Order of the Loyal Legion of the United States, an organization open only to Union officers.

Members included just about all the biggies: Grant, Sherman, Meade, Sheridan, Hancock, Porter. In 1888 the Legion established a Civil War museum in Philadelphia. Members or their descendants wound up donating tons of memorabilia. It all piled up, creating a massive, cluttered repository of

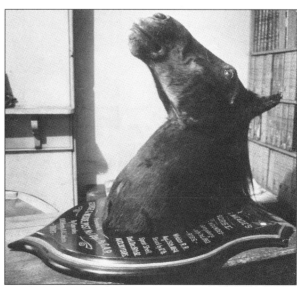

MARILYN A. SHAPIRO

The mounted head of Old Baldy, George G. Meade's favorite horse, is the official mascot of the Civil War Museum & Library.

Individual "escutcheons" represented the military career of Civil War soldiers.

some of the most important historical artifacts of the war.

It became a museum, in the modern sense, only in recent years. For decades a hidebound board of directors ran the place as a sort of private club. There was no staff, no attempt to organize, catalogue or properly display materials that filled every nook and cranny of a four-story townhouse.

Things changed dramatically when full-time, paid director Russ Pritchard took the helm. A Southern-born, nationally known Civil War and military weapons expert, he brought order to the collection, organized a "friends" group and opened the

The Lincoln Room provides a table to study Civil War documents.

treasure chest to the public. Today many experts feel it's the finest collection of Union memorabilia to be found anywhere.

Items still fill every nook, hallway and staircase of the old townhouse dating to 1853. There are even some interesting Civil War items on walls of the Men's Room. But today it's all well organized and professionally displayed. Visitors receive a seven-page, self-guided tour that touches all the highlights of the collection.

Each room contains specialized displays. A Lincoln Room is filled totally with Lincoln memorabilia. There is also a Grant Room, an Armory Room (weapons), a Navy Room, a Confederate Room, a gallery with changing exhibits. A Meade Room is in the making. And a quaint, cozy room labeled "The Dames' Victorian Parlor" is where the wives of the loyal legionnaires gathered while the menfolk told old war stories.

Bookcases found all over the house hold about 12,000 books, manuscripts, regimental histories, diaries and letters plus the 128-volume set containing all governmental war records.

The Lincoln Room has a rather solemn, shrine-like quality. Just reading an original "Wanted" poster offering a $50,000 reward for John Wilkes Booth and $25,000 each for his co-conspirators produced goose bumps.

There's an original handbill for the play "Our American Cousin" at Ford's Theater. There are many photographs and portraits of Lincoln, a huge bust, plaster masks of his face and hands made in life, a lock of his hair, mourning badges, small pieces of bunting cut from Lincoln's box at Ford's Theater and from the pall that covered his casket.

You'll see many items of local interest: a recruiting poster for the Corn Exchange Regiment offering a $160 "bounty" for enlistment and the unit's tattered flag. There is a very large bulletin seeking recruits for a Philadelphia "home guard."

General Grant's dress-uniform jacket still contains a John Wanamaker's label. In excellent shape is a large guidon flag, carried by George Armstrong Custer's unit at Gettysburg.

The common items carried by the soldiers are of particular interest: a folding cup, playing cards, a package of chewing tobacco, rock-like hardtack biscuits, a small "Handbook for U.S. Soldiers," printed in 1861 by Lippincott Publishers of Philadelphia.

General George Meade, who led the Union forces at Gettysburg, lived just around the

Every inch of space displays Civil War memorabilia on Pine Street.

corner from the museum. Meade's horse Old Baldy was almost as famous as the general. Despite numerous battle wounds the faithful steed had nerves of steel under fire. He led every Philadelphia Memorial Day parade and outlived Meade by many years. When Old Baldy died, sentimental veterans dug him up and had his head mounted. Baldy is the museum's mascot; the mounted head of an Army mule is deputy assistant mascot.

The Civil War Museum & Library, 1805 Pine Street. Open 10 a.m. to 4 p.m. Monday through Saturday. Phone: 735-8196

GRAND ARMY OF THE REPUBLIC CIVIL WAR MUSEUM & LIBRARY

The collection here is not quite so large, not as well preserved. But this museum, located in a historic house in Frankford, offers a wonderful bonus. It's filled with friendly volunteer guides in authentic Civil War dress. These folks are real Civil War freaks. Many are "re-enactors" whose idea of a great weekend is fighting the "rebels" with blank cartridges. They're usually well-versed on all the small

Visitors crowd a display case at Frankford's Grand Army of the Republic Museum.

details of Army life and battlefield maneuvers of the 1860s.

The museum is open only one Sunday a month, but in addition to the uniformed guides there are always special events such as lectures, demonstrations, music, or fashion shows of period dress.

The Grand Army of the Republic (GAR) was the largest of all veterans' groups and open to both enlisted men and officers. There were once 36 GAR posts in the city. The bulk of the material here represents the collecting efforts of Post 2, founded immediately after the war and counting Ulysses S. Grant as a dues-paying member.

It wasn't until 1982 that the museum opened its doors to the public and opened its membership rolls to those without ancestors who fought in the Civil War.

It has less weaponry than its Center City counterpart. But it does boast an extensive collection of what might be termed "holy relics," such as a tiny sliver of the bloody

pillowcase from Lincoln's deathbed. More interesting is a pair of handcuffs found among John Wilkes Booth's possessions. His original plans were to capture Lincoln alive and bring him to Richmond for trial. The handcuffs were probably connected to this plot.

There's a brick from Lincoln's box at Ford's Theater, a shingle from Grant's cabin at Appomattox. There's an original witness subpoena for the trial of Booth's co-conspirator David Herold. There's a piece of the Confederate flag that flew over Richmond the day of its capture.

One interesting item is a mangled silver coin that stopped a bullet that hit Brigadier General Gideon Clark. The GAR also snared a good deal of Meade memorabilia: Old Baldy's bridle, Meade's chair and campaign hat. They also have a saddle used by General George McClellan.

Both museums contain small forests of "battle logs," sections of trees sprouting bullets or unexploded shells instead of leaves. The GAR collection has many original uniforms, including an Army greatcoat, caps and the red pants and vest of a Zouave. Many items were taken from the dead, such as Bibles, letters, shoes, Confederate money, daguerreotype portraits.

The museum has the battle flags of 30 Pennsylvania units, a collection considered a great treasure. But the flags are not in good shape and need expensive restoration.

The GAR museum was formerly the house of physician Dr. John Ruan and dates to 1796. It has a 1,200-book library, and visitors are helped to locate ancestors who fought in the war. Both museums have monthly "Round Tables" featuring an author or speaker on some aspect of the Civil War. Both museums are well-worth a visit.

The GAR Museum and Library is at 4278 Griscom Street (Griscom runs parallel to Frankford Avenue). It is open on the first Sunday of the month from noon to 5 p.m. Phone: 289-6484

✳ ✳ ✳ ✳ ✳

HINDA SCHUMAN

A uniformed guide at the GAR museum in Frankford.

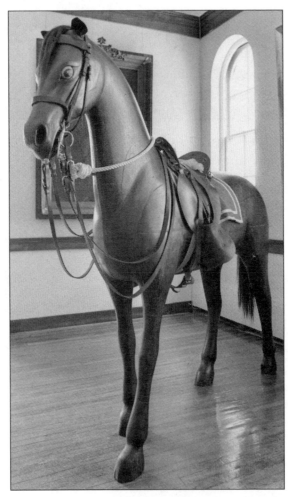

*First City Troop's 19th century wooden horse
for portrait-posing purposes.*

Chapter 14

FAMED AND FABLED
FIGHTING PHILLIES

Everyone knows a National Guard armory is a building where weekend warriors gather, a place to store weapons and military equipment. But in Philadelphia there are two armories proudly boasting impressive military museums.

These armories are packed with history because both units date to the American Revolution and have been making history and saving memorabilia for more than two centuries. Both collections are rich in historic material, professionally displayed and organized. Military history and weapons buffs will find treasures at both places. Both are open to the public by appointment.

The castle-like armory of First City Troop on 23rd Street.

FIRST TROOP
PHILADELPHIA CITY CAVALRY

Both its glorious past and its unique "rights and privileges" make First City Troop the most unusual National Guard unit in the nation. Its founding in 1774 followed the First Continental Congress. Thus it claims to be the oldest American military unit in continuous existence and the first formed specifically to prepare for possible conflict with Great Britain.

The 28 founding members were from among the city's oldest and most respected families. That old Philadelphia blue-blood tradition lingers and is reflected in today's duty roster.

In fact, one almost has to be a gentleman of means to be a weekend warrior in this outfit. All members contribute their National Guard pay to the Troop's treasury. Those who ride in the unit's ceremonial mounted unit shell out as much as $6,000 for the fancy dress uniforms – unless they are lucky enough to inherit the gear.

"Ancient rights and privileges" granted by Congress to militia units that predated the Civil War allows the Troop to elect its own members. The membership then elects its own officers.

Carbines and a manikin in First City Troop's museum room.

The Troop is well-known for its ceremonial duties, archaic dress uniforms and gala social events. But it is also an honest-to-goodness, National Guard unit that switches from saddles to tanks at weekend drills and summer camp.

There's a museumlike quality about the entire armory, but one room has been set aside to display the unit's treasures.

It's a dandy little gem of a museum. The most honored object is its original standard (flag) from 1775. It's one of the few original military flags from the Revolution in existence and appears to be the first American flag to incorporate the use of the 13 blue and white stripes, which appear in one corner with the unit's emblem and motto in the center.

Another rare piece of cloth is the tattered remains of a Hessian battle flag captured at the Battle of Trenton in

The unit emblem is the centerpiece of the City Troop's original flag from 1775.

1776. One hallowed relic, in excellent shape, is a 1777 letter from George Washington thanking the unit for its service and discharging it "for the present."

The museum also features manikins in vintage uniforms, and what might be the most complete collection of cavalry sabres and carbines to be found anywhere.

The collection contains numerous portraits, including one of Washington by Charles Peale Polk. There's a Thomas Eakins painting and a couple of Frederick Remington pieces. There are photographs of the cavalrymen serving in the Spanish-American War, the Mexican border campaign of 1916 and World War I.

The armory also has an extensive archive that includes a good deal of original Civil War material. The Troop claims it was the first

Union force to arrive at Gettysburg, and its scouting reports were the first to detail the large numbers of Confederate forces in the area.

The archive also stores rare 1920s film footage of what is believed to be the last official cavalry charge exercises carried out by the Army.

Two of the most interesting objects in the armory are found in the Troop's dining hall. One is a wooden horse from the late 19th century used to practice mounting and for posing purposes. Covering much wall space is a massive, 16-foot-long portrait of every member of the 1899 Troop mounted on horseback. Obviously, the entire unit didn't sit in the saddle for weeks posing for artist Carl Becker, who worked from individual portraits.

The First City Troop Armory is at 23rd and Ranstead Streets. Museum open by appointment only. Phone: 564-1488.

103RD ENGINEERS

It hardly seems possible, but the 103rd Engineers have seen more action and collected more war relics and memorabilia than the First City Troop.

Its name and function has changed several times since it was organized to defend Philadelphia in 1777. But it never disbanded. The same unit, the same personnel, just assumed different identities. It fought from Germantown to Yorktown in the War of Independence. It was called up for the War of 1812, the Mexican War of 1845, the Civil War, the Spanish-American, World War I, World War II. It spent the Korean War on active duty in Germany.

In between major wars, it was called out for the Whiskey Rebellion of 1793; it guarded Harrisburg in the so-called Buckshot War of 1838. It put down full-scale riots between Irish

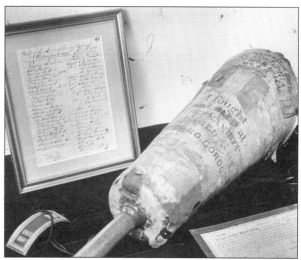

Among items on display at the 103rd Engineers museum is the wooden leg that replaced a limb lost at Buena Vista in the Mexican War.

Catholics and native Protestants in South Philadelphia in 1844, when it sustained two dead and 23 injured.

At the turn of the century it was shipped to Pittsburgh to put down labor violence in the steel mills. When Mexican bandit Pancho Villa raided across the border in 1915, the same gang of Philadelphians was sent to Texas, where the only injuries recorded came from kicking mules.

It started as an artillery unit and took the name "Washington Grays," because of its close association with George Washington. In the Civil War it became an infantry unit, known as the Gray Reserves. It is a statue of a Gray Reserve soldier that stands guard in front of the venerable Union League Club on Broad Street. After the conflict it was reorganized as the First Regiment Infantry, Pennsylvania Militia and took the nickname "The Dandy First." It kept that designation until 1921 when it was converted into a combat engineering unit.

With all the activity, it piled up enough memorabilia to create a museum wing in its sprawling West Philadelphia armory.

Unlike the First City Troop, the engineers have few Revolutionary War mementos – exceptions are a British Brown Bess musket and an Army discharge signed by George Washington and kept locked away in a safe.

But it has an entire room filled with Civil War (and some Mexican War) relics. Another, even larger, room is filled with World War I items. A third room for World War II is slowly taking shape.

A long hallway is lined with glass display cases holding more than a dozen manikins dressed in reproductions of the unit's uniforms from 1777 to 1980. A large foyer is filled with unit awards.

The Civil War Room includes ceremonial swords, weapons, a captured Confederate flag, a shoe left behind by a retreating rebel at Appomattox, recruiting posters, photos, original uniforms, a Springfield musket made at the Frankford Arsenal with an elaborate hand-carved stock. One of the most interesting items is an official presidential ballot of the Confederate States with Jefferson Davis' name on top. Items predating the Civil War include an 1845 photo of a Washington Gray soldier and the wooden leg of a Mexican War veteran.

The World War I collection is particularly rich, with hundreds of items ranging from gas

Memorabilia from World War I include uniforms and paintings.

One entire room is filled with souvenirs of the Great War.

masks to machine guns to a large artillery piece. The many small personal items on display include the pocket-sized "Kolynos Parley Voo Booklet" containing "Practical French and German Phrases and how to Pronounce Them."

There's a captured pack of German "Salem Aleikum" cigarettes and a German "turtle trap." Pick up the palm-sized canister and it explodes.

The outfit lost 745 men in the Great World War. Against Hitler, the Engineers landed at Normandy, got caught in the opening phase of the Battle of the Bulge, crossed the Rhine and fought its way through Germany as part of the 28th Infantry Division.

There are Engineers who will argue that their unit is even older than the First City Troop. Its first commander, Jehu Eyre and several members had been "Associators," the militia started by Ben Franklin in 1747. But let the horse cavalry and the engineers fight this one out with sabres and wooden horses.

The 103rd Engineers Armory is at 33rd and Lancaster Avenue. Call ahead for an appointment to see the museum. Phone: 823-4901

✳ ✳ ✳ ✳ ✳

The distinctive Spanish architecture of the
Samuel Yellin workshop built in 1915.

Chapter 15

A COMPANY WITH MANY
IRONS IN THE FIRE
Samuel Yellin Metalworkers Company

A blacksmith is supposed to be a big, grunting, hairy-armed galoot who bends iron bars with fire and muscle. Sam Yellin was a blacksmith who pounded his anvil to a different beat.

A photograph shows the Polish-born Yellin hammering a white-hot bar, wearing an artist's smock, white shirt and tie while professorially puffing a briar pipe.

Yellin happened to be an educated man who lectured at the University of Pennsylvania, wrote encyclopedia articles on blacksmithing and was, himself, the subject of articles in art magazines.

He was a blacksmith who endowed his work with such artistic inspiration that "Yellin Ironwork" became a synonym – like Tiffany and Rolls Royce – for perfection and luxury. Every millionaire wanted original Yellin ironwork to show off in his mansion.

Yellin died in 1940, but the anvils continue to ring in his West Philadelphia shop under the leadership of his daughter-in-law Marian and granddaughter, Clare Yellin.

Part of the shop is a very unusual museum displaying the one-of-kind ornamental metal pieces and painstaking craftsmanship which have all but vanished.

But it's more than a collection of what is probably the most artistic ironwork of 20th century America. Marian Yellin gives a detailed guided tour of a very unique business, which includes a trip to the work floor and often a chat with the current master blacksmith.

In some ways, the place is exactly what one expects of a metal shop: old, grimy, cluttered with tools and equipment, full of glowing coal hearths and sweaty workers bending, twisting and hammering hot metal.

But Samuel Yellin's office is something no one would expect in an industrial workshop. It's like a room lifted from a medieval European castle. Yellin's great love and inspiration in art were the classic Gothic styles.

In the late 1920s he traveled to Europe at the request of his admirer and patron, millionaire Edward Bok, to buy art objects to fill the soon to open Philadelphia Museum of Art. Yellin had a few bucks of his own and also purchased medieval art and furnishings for himself.

So, his office has the feel of a museum, boasting a 400-year-old Elizabethean recliner chair, an equally old and impressive antique table, handsome sea chests with fancy iron fittings. Ancient tapestries hang on the walls.

Some metal objects in the office were made by Yellin, but fit right into the medieval setting. One wall contains a large, castle-like fireplace with an intricately designed wrought iron grating that Yellin, a perfectionist, considered his most perfect work.

The museum showrooms are chock-full of delicate, very intricate wrought iron and some bronze pieces. Most are "fragments" saved from major jobs. There are stairway railings, lamps, candlestick holders, fireplace screens, grates, doors, door knockers, fences, candle sconces, huge locks and ornamental hardware. Many pieces have interesting stories attached to them, and Yellin's daughter-in-law is fond of recalling the details.

Yellin's work was strictly for the few who could afford the huge investment in time and labor that such work requires: millionaires, banks, colleges, churches and major institutions. Visitors are always amazed when Marian Yellin quotes prices: $28,000 for one chandelier. Yes, but the price tag reflects almost 900 hours of labor.

Yellin's first major commission was a gate for the J.P. Morgan estate on Long Island in 1911. The other barons of industry soon came calling on the craftsman. Yellin gates, railings and other objects were purchased for the estates of Rockefellers, Vanderbilts, Fords, DuPonts, Mellon, Astor, Eastman and many Main Line patricians.

Colleges sporting Yellin ironwork include Yale, Princeton, Penn, Bowdoin, Bryn Mawr, Pittsburgh, Cornell and Columbia. Many banks and office buildings sought Yellin work. One of the largest jobs was 200 tons of fancy iron-

work, costing $260,000 in the early 1920s, for the Federal Reserve Bank in New York City.

The company has been making railings, gates and grills for the slow-rising "National" Cathedral in Washington, D.C. for decades.

In Philadelphia, famous Yellin works include the gate at St. Mark's Church at 16th and Locust; the Academy of Music's door frames; Curtis Institute of Music; gates and doors and the grates, grills, railings, lighting fixtures and benches of the Packard Building at 15th and Chestnut.

While there are other ornamental iron firms in the city – and scores in the early 1900s – Yellin's work was always different. He'd never touch cast iron. All items were, and still are, handcrafted, with Yellin craftsmen working from individual sketches and drawings.

Today Yellin is among the last firms doing this sort of expensive handwork. And today there is no such thing as real wrought iron. The raw material of wrought iron is no longer manufactured in America. Today Yellin blacksmiths use a similar product called "mild iron."

During its heyday in the 1920s, Samuel Yellin employed about 200, and just about all his skilled artisans were trained in Europe. The work force is down to about 10 craftsmen (many are art school graduates) and a part-time designer.

Yellin's clients are still a Who's Who of the nation's elite – people who blithely shell out thousands for artsy items and hardware that lend touches of opulence and class to a house.

The shop, itself, is a strange, one-of-a-kind, Spanish-style building, listed in the National Historic Register and designed for Yellin in 1915 by the famed architects Mellow, Meigs and Howe.

Samuel Yellin Metalworkers Co. is at 5520 Arch Street. Free tours are given by appointment only. No tours during the winter months. Phone: 472-3122

* * * * *

The workshop floor and some fragments of Yellin ironwork.

The second home of papermaker Wilhelm Rettinghaus was completed in 1713.

Chapter 16

THE VILLAGE PEOPLE

RittenhouseTown

Occasionally the astute motorist notices on major, old, arterial streets – Bustleton or Ridge avenues, for example – a tiny cluster of old houses dating to the 18th or 19th centuries.

They are vestiges of small villages and cross-road hamlets that fused together and were swallowed up by municipal sprawl and political consolidation.

Amazingly, one of those quiet, rural villages survives (partly) in the modern asphalt jungle. It's scenic, quaint, charming. It's 300-year-old RittenhouseTown on Lincoln Drive.

If they hadn't been added to the Fairmount Park system more than 100 years ago, those charming, old houses would certainly now be in the hands of trendy boutique and fern bar entrepreneurs, creating a dreadful New Hope-on-the-Wissahickon.

A group called Friends of Historic Rittenhouse Town Inc. is busy trying to preserve, protect and promote this forgotten little gem as a tourist attraction. For the time being, there are few visitors, so it's still a bit of country tranquillity in the city.

True, very little of the village still stand. Only seven of 40 buildings that once included a mill, school, church and firehouse, survive. Still those seven historic houses are enough to preserve the cozy feel of a village.

Miraculously, the original home of German-immigrant papermaker Wilhelm Rettinghaus, built in 1690, remains. It's a simple, one-room affair with a huge fireplace (said to be the largest in Pennsylvania) and it's as solid as the day it was built.

Rettinghaus, later anglicized to Rittenhouse, was America's first papermaker and the nation's first Mennonite minister. If the paper industry were sentimental about these things, the little village would be a national shrine.

It remained an important papermaking center until the middle of the 19th century when wood pulp paper replaced linen-based stock. The original Rettinghaus home was replaced by a much larger Georgian-style dwelling in 1707, and this too remains in wonderful shape. Here the most famous Rittenhouse, David, was born. A close chum of Ben Franklin and Tom Jefferson, David

Rittenhouse was an ingenious clockmaker, astronomer, mathematican and all-around man of science.

One of the most interesting aspects of the second Rittenhouse home is a round, wooden plug in its rear door. The site was no-man's-land between the Red Coats and Washington's Army in 1777. The plug was needed to repair a musketball hole from the Revolutionary War.

To the left of the front door is a door that seems to go nowhere. Known as the "death door," it was used only when someone in the house died, to remove the corpse. According to German superstition, the spirit of the dead person was thus barred from re-entering the premises.

Another surviving structure is a barn currently used for papermaking demonstrations. All the houses are solid stone structures with thick walls and date to the 18th century with later modifications.

The homes are leased, mostly to city employees, under the sound philosophy that full-time residents provide a degree of protection from vandals and arsonists. Those lucky enough to live in RittenhouseTown say the feel and ambience is like true country living. In the cold months there are few two-footed visitors. Raccoons, possums, deer and wild ducks are abundant.

The houses line the gentle Monoshone Creek, which joins the Wissahickon a few hundred yards away. The first Rittenhouse mill was destroyed by a flood just 10 years after it was built. The second mill was torn down in the 1890s, but archaeologists have recently uncovered parts of the foundation.

The Rittenhouses were a prolific clan. More than 500 descendants of Wilhelm Rettinghaus recently gathered for a reunion. Living less than two blocks from the ancestral home is retiree Clem Rittenhouse, a ninth generation descendant. He takes frequent strolls into the village where his father was born and where he played and swam as a youngster.

You don't have to be a history-buff to appreciate this bucolic slice of the city. Anyone with a little feeling for beauty will find a visit rewarding.

RittenhouseTown is located along Lincoln Drive at Rittenhouse Street. The two original Rittenhouse homes are open for tours on Saturdays, April through October from 10 a.m. to 4 p.m. There are special weekend open-houses and events during the spring and summer.

✳ ✳ ✳ ✳ ✳

The bucolic stillness is reflected in the gentle creek that flows through historic RittenhouseTown.

*The Fleisher Art Memorial is a collection
of adjoining buildings, including a former
Episcopal Church built in 1886.*

Chapter 17

HIGH ART IN MUMMER COUNTRY
Samuel S. Fleisher Art Memorial

This is another of those marvelous surprises that makes South Philadelphia the most interesting and appealing neighborhood in the city. Just a tomato-throw from the boisterous outdoor Ninth Street Italian Market is an oasis of tranquillity and aesthetic delight.

The name is misleading. It's not an "art memorial." It's a free art school established in 1898 by Samuel S. Fleisher, an art-worshipping, idealistic, millionaire woolens manufacturer. It was first called "the Graphic Sketch Club" and it claims to be the oldest free art school in the nation. It's probably the best too.

By conservative estimate, 50 percent of all professional Philadelphia artists of this century have studied here at some point. Evenings the place is packed with adults painting, drawing and sculpting, mostly for

MARILYN A. SHAPIRO

The stained glass wheel window in the Sanctuary was made in Holland.

the joy of it. It's an odd student mix. Firemen and welfare mothers stand easel-to-easel with those holding degrees from top art colleges.

What makes the school worth a visit are its changing gallery shows of area artists and, especially, a unique space called "The Sanctuary."

The school is composed of five adjoining 19th century buildings (making it hard to find the proper entrance). One structure was a charity called "St. Martin's College for Indigent Boys." Two are brick rowhouses dating to the 1870s. But the centerpiece is a unique former Episcopal church completed in 1886 and now "The Sanctuary." For those who can't afford to fly to Italy to tour the ancient churches, "The Sanctuary" provides a close approximation.

When Dr. Henry Robert Percival (1854-1903) took the pulpit of the Church of the Evangelist

Samuel Fleisher commissioned a statue and altarpiece of Moses for his Sanctuary.

in 1880, it was a dying parish. Percival was a dynamic leader of the Oxford Movement, which aimed to harmonize the Episcopal and Roman Catholic churches.

Percival replaced the existing church with one ancient in design, as a symbol of Christianity's changelessness. He reached back 1,000 years for his architectural models.

The firm of famed Philadelphia architect Frank Furness drew up the plans, based on characteristics of several different Italian churches, dating from A.D. 900 to 1,400. Percival obviously attracted a moneyed class to his parish. Marble was imported from Italy. Henry Mercer's tile works made special tile, which have since disappeared. A Samuel Yellin wrought iron grate was added to the front door.

Outside, two lumps of stone, which appear to be lions worn by centuries of time and weather, enhance the ancient image. Inside, walls were painted with medieval-style religious scenes. One muralist was Robert Henri, one of the city's most renowned artists. The paintings are not true frescoes and have become quite faded, which only enhances the Old World feel. Stained glass windows were made by masters of the craft in England and by local stained glass artist Nicola D'Ascenzo.

After Percival's death, the congregation declined and the church folded. The neighborhood became the heart of Philadelphia's Italian-immigrant community. Fleisher's Sketch Club had already relocated next door in the former school for "indigent boys" when he purchased the abandoned church in 1922.

Fleisher did more than save an exquisite building. He left enough money after his death in 1944 to fill his "Sanctuary" with museum quality Medieval and Renaissance church art worth millions.

It's amazing to encounter all these Old Masters in such a little-known place. Art lovers who have already visited the biggies such as the Pennsylvania Academy of the Fine Arts should make Fleisher their next stop.

Among the most valuable objects are two large paintings of four back-to-back saints, dating to 1490, by Spanish master Pablo Vergos. There are several Madonna and Child paintings. A work done in 1480 is credited to a chap known as the "The Master of Budapest." The Sanctuary also has statues of the saints dating to the 13th and 14th centuries. There are old Russian icons, wood carvings, a Florentine altar, and a 15th century French abbot's chair – last used by artist Lois Nevelson during a 1985 visit.

Not every work of art is of ancient origin. Fleisher commissioned local artist, Violet Oakley to paint a large reredos or altar piece depicting the life of Moses. He also commissioned a bronze statue of Moses by sculptor J. Wallace Kelly.

The Sanctuary is used for inspiration, meditation, lectures, concerts and an occasional wedding.

The Fleisher student who achieved the greatest success and fame was an immigrant boy from Estonia named Louis Kahn. As a teenager, Kahn walked miles from his home in North Philadelphia to attend the art classes. He became one of America's most influential modern architects but always maintained a warm, close relationship with the school.

MARILYN A. SHAPIRO

A medieval carving of a bishop in limestone.

The Sanctuary is the scene for an occasional concert.

A stark but fascinating meeting room honors former Fleisher student Louis Kahn.

A door in the Sanctuary leads directly into the Louis Kahn Lecture Room, a jolting 1,000-year trip in style. The room was designed by Iranian-born artist Siah Armajani to honor Kahn by incorporating his ideas.

There's not much to the room: benches, a platform with a speaker's stand, two windows with odd shutters, a quote carved into the floorboards, another quote overhead.

The room was meant to be functional and is used for lectures or small art shows. It is also supposed to make a visitor think. And it certainly does that. There's a strange, disorienting quality about the room. Everything seems slight askew, asymmetrical.

The Samuel S. Fleischer Art Memorial is at 709-721 Catharine Street. Galleries and the Sanctuary are opened September through June, Monday to Friday, noon to 5 p.m. and during school hours Monday through Thursdays 6:30 p.m. to 9:30 p.m. Phone: 922-3456

✳ ✳ ✳ ✳ ✳

Chapter 18

TWO ODDBALLS
FROM SOUTH PHILLY

There are probably a lot of strange sights in South Philadelphia but two structures – both oddly out of character with their surroundings and apparently abandoned – are puzzling. One appears to be a massive Greek temple, the other a weird tower of some sort. Both provide rather interesting historical yarns and both are allegedly haunted by ghosts.

THE RIDGWAY LIBRARY

Like the Schuylkill Expressway, this mammoth structure on South Broad Street was a controversial pain-in-the-neck from Day One. More than a century after its erection, it's still a headache.

The story of Philadelphia's own Parthenon begins – like almost everything else in this city – with Ben Franklin. Ben and some brainy buddies formed a discussion group called "the Junta," which led in 1731 to the founding of America's first private "subscription" library, called the Philadelphia Library Company.

The library grew and grew, moving to several locations including a room in Independence Hall.

One of this library's directors in the 19th century was Dr. James Rush, a son of the famous Philadelphia physician and Declaration of Independence signer, Dr. Benjamin Rush.

Dr. James, also a physician, was a reclusive bookworm and sourpuss who married a rich, jolly fat lady, Phoebe Anne Ridgway, proving once again that opposites do attract. Mrs. Rush died in 1857, and Dr. Rush decided he would leave most of her fortune to build a new home for the Library Company.

He drew up a fairly simple seven-page will in 1860, but kept adding new instructions on how he wanted things done. By the time Rush died in 1869, the will was up to 35 pages.

Among its myriad provisions was the demand that the new library building be named "Ridgway" to honor his wife and father-in-law. Also, he and his wife were to be entombed in the building – a Philly fad started by Stephen Girard, entombed at Girard College.

Rush's instructions forbade cushioned seats, to discourage loafing. He didn't want any lectures or social events held in his library. He went further: the library was not to be "encumbered with ephemeral biographies, novels and works of fiction or amusements, newspapers or periodicals." All this might have been acceptable. After all, Rush had left $1 million, an enormous sum for the time.

The executor of the will, however, was Rush's brother-in-law, Henry J. Williams, who proved to be as stubborn and eccentric as Rush. Williams decided to build the library where no one wanted it: in South Philly, away from Center City and the library's membership.

The Library Company went to court over the location and lost a two-year battle. The ill-feeling was so great, a vote was held on whether to accept the $1 million or tell Williams to take the cash and shove it. By a slender five-vote margin, the gift was accepted, 298-to-293 with another 350 members abstaining.

The building opened in 1878. It was, and still is, a most imposing edifice. But from the start the roof leaked. The basement flooded. And it was freezing cold in winter. How do you heat such a massive space?

Then there was the matter of the ghost. The couple's crypt was in a separate room, but janitors claimed to encounter ghosts wandering about at night.

Worst of all, no one came. There was a second Library Company branch at 13th and Locust, and that's where everybody went. Two or three visitors a day became the norm at Ridgway. Smart alecks started calling Ridgway "Philadelphia's largest mausoleum." Even in the 1920s there was talk of dumping it. The roof still leaked and the temperature never got above 50 degrees in the winter.

During the Depression, the Library Company closed its Locust Street branch, and that brought more readers to Broad Street. In the 1940s, the cost of maintaining the place was so high, shareholders allowed the City Free Library to operate the place and opened it to the general public.

In the 1950s, the Library Company almost unloaded the building on the city as headquarters for the police department. Wiser heads argued that a cavernous, granite Greek temple was not an ideal setup for modern police administration. One idea was to convert it into a replacement for obsolete Moyamensing Prison.

The city finally purchased the 3.5-acre property in 1964 for $675,000. It has has been trying to figure out what to do with its empty temple ever since.

Part of the basement and the rear grounds are used as a city recreation center, but 80 percent of the building remains an empty shell, neglected and forlorn. One entrepreneur put forward the novel proposal of turning it into a disco. Certain school officials have their eyes on it as a home for the High School for Performing Arts.

In the meantime, the venerable Library Company is back again on Locust Street near 13th in up-to-date digs – heat in the winter, air conditioning in summer. They even brought the Rushes and their crypt to the new home.

The Library Company is among Philadelphia's greatest treasures, with 450,000 books,

The tomb and remains of Dr. James Rush and Phoebe Anne Ridgway Rush now rest at the Library Company's Locust Street facility.

Vacant and forlorn, the old Ridgway Library building on South Broad Street.

MARILYN A. SHAPIRO

160,000 manuscripts and a burgeoning collection of historical photos. For $20 anyone can become a shareholder just like Ben Franklin or Dr. Rush.

The Ridgway Library is on Broad Street between Carpenter and Christian Streets.

SPARKS SHOT TOWER

The best view, of what for decades was the tallest structure along the Delaware River waterfront, can be had from your car window as you ride down Route I-95. It's not a smokestack with a lid. It's not a lighthouse nor a silo. It's a Shot Tower. It requires a smattering of physics and a vague knowledge of the Embargo Act of 1807 to tell this tale.

According to some law of physics — you won't get an explanation of it here — molten lead will form into perfect round spheres when dropped from a height. The principle revolutionized the making of gun shot. Instead of the slow, old method of pouring lead into wooden molds, one could build a high tower. The molten lead was then poured through a screenlike device at the top of the tower, falling into a tub of water below. Different sized holes in the screen created different sizes of shot.

Now for the Embargo Act. During the Napoleonic Wars, both England and France started seizing neutral shipping headed for enemy ports. President Jefferson and Congress were so enraged, a law was passed banning all exports. This was supposed to bring the two belligerents to their senses by cutting off American goods. It was, in fact, the classic case of cutting off one's nose to spite the face. America suffered most.

This brings us to a plumber, Thomas Sparks, who was out hunting birds in the swamps in South Philly. The Embargo Act had driven up the cost of lead shot because most had come from Great Britain. An idea sparked in the mind of Sparks: Why not build an American shot tower?

Sparks and two partners found someone who had worked in a British shot tower to guide construction, which began on July 4, 1808. The brickmasons created a 142-foot high tower with a 30-foot base circumference tapering to 15 feet at the top.

It was America's first shot tower, Philadelphia's highest structure. But try to be first with the most in America and there's always a Donald Trump-like figure to top you. The following year, 1809, a fellow named Paul Beck built a larger, higher tower (166 feet) around 21st and Arch.

It was said that Philadelphia's two shot towers could provide enough ammo for all of America plus Asia. Business was good for both places during the War of 1812; but in 1828, Beck packed it in. Demand was only a fraction of his 20-ton daily capacity. His tower eventually was demolished.

The Sparks Tower was worked to capacity during the Civil War. Additional buildings on the site turned out conical bullets in later years. Four generations of the Sparks family kept the tower in operation until 1903, when it was sold to a company that never used it.

The city purchased the site in 1913 and turned the surrounding ground into a playground to serve a very poor, crowded immigrant neighborhood. For reasons that are not clear the city lopped about 10 feet off the height of the tower.

Those who know about such things say the brickwork and general workmanship of the shot tower is superb. An 1875 book on city industries claims the tower was a model for lighthouses: "Members of the United States Lighthouse Board have frequently repaired to its site to copy the model and afterward re-embody it in a lighthouse."

A gymnasium has been built around the base of the tower. Windows were bricked-in and the entrance sealed. A custodian says it's impossible to get inside the tower.

Probably the last time anyone climbed inside and tried to make shot occurred in March 1964. As told by Evening Bulletin columnist James Smart, members of the Poor Richard Club obtained permission to enter the tower through a small trapdoor in the ceiling. Opening the door produced a shower of dust, dirt, feathers and dead pigeons. The spiral staircase was gone, but a metal ladder led to a wooden platform about three stories high.

An intrepid climber carrying lead, a ladle and a propane stove proceeded to try to make shot. "Some sand was spread on the floor," Smart wrote. "The lead was dripped down from above. It formed balls which were imperfect, to put it kindly. They were full of sand too."

A word of caution for any daredevil thinking of climbing the tower. In 1920, neighbors told a reporter the tower was inhabited by an evil-tempered ghost who delights in pushing fools trying to climb it to their deaths.

The Sparks Shot Tower is located in the city playground between Second and Front Streets at Carpenter Street.

MARILYN A. SHAPIRO

A waterfront landmark since 1808:
the Sparks Shot Tower.

Chapter 19

MUSEUMS: TOOTH AND NAIL

An entire book could be written about Philadelphia's place in medical history. The University of Pennsylvania opened the nation's first medical school. The Philadelphia College of Pharmacy and Science was the first pharmacy school in the Western Hemisphere and both have interesting historical displays.

Thomas Jefferson University is historic and has produced more physicians than any other American medical school. It owns what many consider the greatest American painting of all time: Thomas Eakins' wonderful "Gross Clinic." By all means, see it.

The Mutter Museum of the Philadelphia College of Physicians offers a thousand delights for those fascinated by skulls, spines, spleens, pickled brains, body parts and medical gear in general. Here we examine a couple of the more obscure medical attractions in town.

THE FOOT MUSEUM

You'll have to walk many-a-mile to find a more prestigious and comprehensive collection of historic and exotic footwear than that displayed by the proud podiatrists of the Pennsylvania College of Podiatric Medicine. Yes, we're talking celebrity footwear, shoes in art and literature and ethnic foot fashion from mukluks to Victorian roller skates.

It's not really a museum, and it's certainly not on the "A" list of Philadelphia tourist attractions. On the other hand (make that the other foot), it's not as weird and dull as one

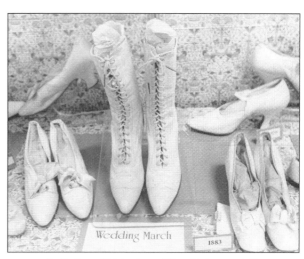

A display of historic wedding footware at the Pennsylvania College of Podiatric Medicine.

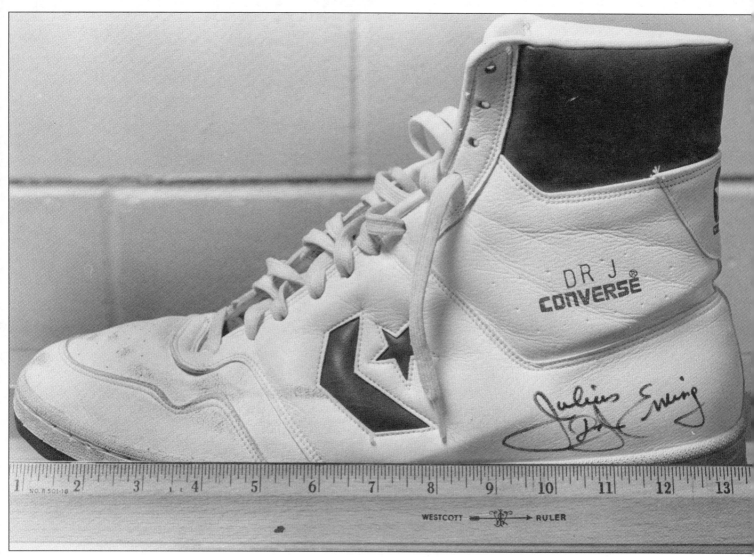

The gunboat-sized sneaker of Julius "Dr. J" Erving.

might expect. The guided tour provided by the very knowledgeable part-time curator is surprisingly interesting. You'll come away knowing the origin of the word "sabotage" and dozens of other intriguing foot facts to amaze and delight your friends.

The collection is housed in glass display cases on the sixth floor of the podiatry school. A good portion of the collection is on permanent loan from the Mutter Museum and most other items have been donated by foot doctors and shoe sellers.

The visitor will certainly get a kick out of footwear that once covered the toes of the rich and famous. You can gaze upon the jazzy, multicolored shoes of Ringo Starr. There's a boot that was part of Sandy Duncan's "Peter Pan" outfit and one of Lucille Ball's dress

shoes. Joe Frazier's boxing shoes are amazingly long and narrow and Julius Erving's basketball sneakers are, not surprisingly, humongous. Yes Flyers' fans, the collection proudly displays one of goalie Bernie Parent's own ice skates.

Moving on to footwear oddities, there's a size 18-D once worn by a circus tall man and an immense gunboat of a shoe worn by a woman with the disease of gigantism. There's a display of worldwide ethnic footwear, including the tiny, tiny shoes worn by Chinese women subjected to footbinding. Still another case, labeled "The Foolish Foot," features fashions that are murder on the tootsies such as ridiculously high spiked heels.

And there's more to see: the dress shoes of First Ladies Mamie Eisenhower, Betty Ford and

Nancy Reagan – not to mention a black, laceless shoe worn by the old Gipper. The worn slipper of a Pennsylvania Ballet Company member provides graphic evidence of the tootsie-torture ballet folks endure.

The collection includes printed material, such as old books on foot care and shoemaking. Want to learn the colorful calls of 19th century itinerant corn-cutters? Here's an opportunity to learn the words.

The Pennsylvania College of Podiatric Medicine is at 8th and Race streets. Free tours for groups or individuals can be arranged in advance. Phone: 629-0300.

TEMPLE'S DENTAL MUSEUM

This won't hurt you a bit. It is considered one of the great dental collections of the world. And sometime in late 1991, it will finally get the display space it so richly deserves.

There's a lot of glorious dental history here. Temple University's dental school was once the Philadelphia College of Dentistry, America's second oldest dental school founded in 1863. (Baltimore beat Philadelphia for this First by more than 20 years.)

Over the decades, the school amassed enough dental artifacts to fill several rooms, spill into the hallway, and still have thousands of unseen items in storage. The school has never had the space to show off the collection properly, but with the opening of a new wing to the dental school, there's space to create a true museum.

You don't have to be a member of the American Academy of the History of Dentistry (there is such a group) to enjoy this place. There's a lot of important stuff here, such as the oldest surviving American dentist chair, dating to about 1790. And there are a lot of interesting tooth oddities, including a display case

America's oldest dental chair at Temple University's Dental Museum.

devoted to America's most flamboyant dentist, Edgar "Painless" Parker.

During a 60-year career, Painless yanked thousands of teeth and apparently saved most. Some he strung into necklaces. The rest he threw into an old wooden bucket. Temple has Parker's brimming bucket of teeth – an impressive sight.

There's a nice collection of the skulls and jawbones and facial models with removable teeth used to train student dentists. There are many historic dentists' chairs and footpowered dental drills. One 1850s-model chair is a nice, cushioned easy chair fitted with head and footrests. Another chair has a coal foot warmer.

One intriguing device from the 1890s is a primitive battery used to zap the poor patient to "raise the threshold of pain" during root canal.

The visitor will gaze upon an impressive collection of ivory handled 18th century "extraction keys," wonderful instruments of torture for removing stubborn teeth. There's a display case full of historic boar and badger bristle toothbrushes, ivory tongue scrapers and vintage silk dental floss. Of course the collection includes a root of the arrack tree, which has served admirably as a toothbrush for the ancient and modern peoples of the Middle East.

Visitors can read scores of newspaper ads of 18th and 19th century dentists or enjoy early

A few thousand of the many teeth pulled by "Painless Parker" during a 60-year career.

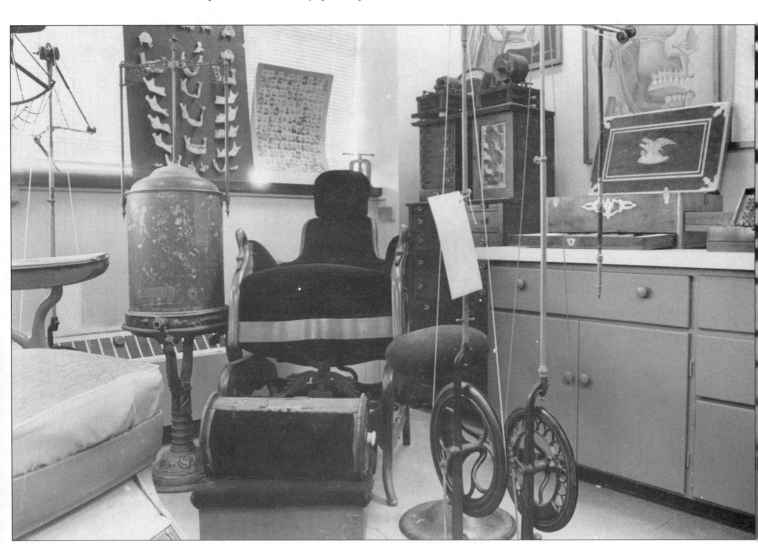

Foot-powered drills and a dental chair with a foot warmer at Temple.

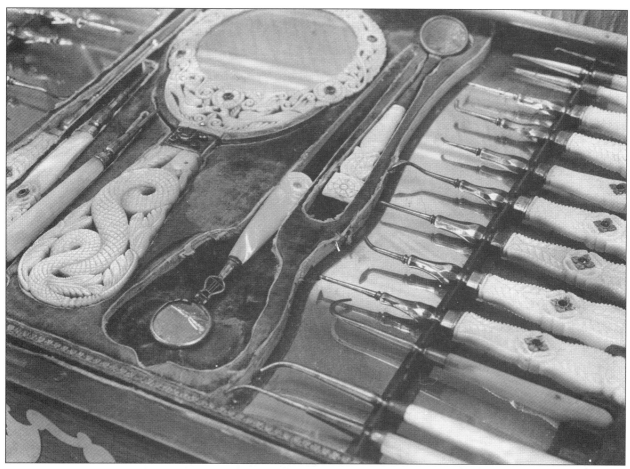
A handsome Civil War era dental kit.

cartoons depicting dental tortures. There is also a fine Medieval-era painting of St. Appollonia, patron saint of the dental profession. This early Christian martyr had her teeth knocked out.

Yes, you'll see early X-ray machines, Civil War era dental kits and handy-dandy "scarificators," small razor-sharp devices used in bleeding patients.

The Temple Dental Museum is located in the Dental School at Broad and Alleghany. Best to call ahead. Phone: 221-2816

✳ ✳ ✳ ✳ ✳

The city's only log cabin is on a small street in Northern Liberties.

Chapter 20

URBAN HOMESTEADS
OF DISTINCTION

The booster who coined the phrase "City of Homes," to describe Philadelphia, hit upon a basic truth.

Philadelphians love their homes. They invest loads of imagination, care and labor on the simplest rowhouses. Even as these words are written, the author is being serenaded by the energetic hammering of carpenters adding a costly deck to a neighbor's house, an embellishment that will provide a panoramic view of our concrete, trash-can-lined, rear driveway. This chapter focuses on three proud Philadelphia home-owners and their untypical homes.

LOG CABIN

You can't miss the distinctive house built by the sweat and labor of Jeff Thomas and his wife, Joyce Brenner Thomas, on narrow Lawrence

MARILYN A. SHAPIRO
Basic log cabin construction.

Street in the old Northern Liberties neighborhood.

It's the only log cabin on the block. As a matter of fact, it's the only log cabin in Philadelphia.

Jeff, an artist who pays the bills by house painting, spent 10 years in a log cabin high atop an inaccessible, forested mountain in West Virginia.

He need never pine for his rustic Appalachian homestead. He has not only duplicated the cabin in the middle of old rowhouses, he has also created a wild, woodsy setting to surround it.

The couple met while studying at the Philadelphia College of Art. Jeff took Joyce to his West Virginia cabin, and she too was enraptured by the cozy joys of cabin living.

The couple purchased four rubble-filled lots on Lawrence Street at a city auction in the

There's a nice rural coziness inside the log cabin.

early 1980s. A bit of research proved that an all-wood house is perfectly legal in the city as long as the structure is free-standing.

Of course a lot of the Thomases' gentrifying neighbors felt a log cabin didn't fit well with their own rehab plans, but by the time the gentry organized an opposition, it was too late. Jeff already had his building permits.

With the aid of a laborer, an electrician and a plumber, the couple had the two-story cabin built in a year. The total cost was under $50,000. The basic raw material was 100 sturdy poplar trees cut on a friend's West Virginia spread and shipped to Philly. The logs are notched together, Daniel Boone style, and the spaces chinked with cement. "It's a very basic form of construction," says Jeff. "All the logs go up before you cut out the windows and doors."

The cabin has a rough, primitive look from the outside. But inside there's a wonderfully rustic, cozy feel. The warm country flavor is enhanced by the style of decoration. An ax leans against one wall. A lantern hangs from a beam. A wood-burning stove sits in the middle of the living room; on the stove sits a cast iron kettle. Country hats hang from wall pegs. In addition to a wood-burning stove, there is electric baseboard heat. A fire sprinkler system was installed for insurance purposes.

The couple's backyard has a wild back-to-nature feel. It's filled with wild flowers, creepers, weeds, honeysuckle, morning glories and more than 20 transplanted trees from West

A view from a window in the log cabin.

*Except for a few chairs and a table
the backyard grows wild.*

Virginia. The yard is closed off from public view, creating a postage-stamp sized wilderness that attracts all kinds of birds.

Friends say a visit with the Thomases is like a trip to Maine. Strangers often knock to ask questions. One man offered to buy the cabin on the spot. And once a tour bus from New Jersey drove down Lawrence Street just to give riders a gander at "urban pioneers" who took that phrase to its literal extreme.

The log cabin is on the 800 block of Lawrence, just off 5th and Poplar streets.

LUCKY RAY'S "COUNTRY MANOR"

Many people have been fortunate enough to build their "dream house" in the suburbs or country. But no one ever thought of putting the house of their dreams on the spot Raymond Walter "Lucky Ray" Thompson selected.

Just a few minutes drive separates gentrified Northern Liberties and the rustic cabin from, arguably, the most devastated slum in the city. The neighborhood just east of Broad Street between Girard Avenue and Spring Garden is called "East Poplar" and most of it is pure wasteland.

Many streets have only two or three crumbling houses still standing. The vista is one

The second-floor bedroom in the log cabin.

of rubble-filled empty lots and back alleys, ankle-deep in garbage. Mangy dogs wander the street. Derelicts stand around trash fires in the winter passing a bottle.

Yet if one is looking for wide open spaces and cheap land, this locale is ideal – and only a 15-minute walk to City Hall. This is the nightmare landscape that Thompson chose for his "country estate."

Thompson's manor leaps out at the passerby and screams for attention. A lot of motorists driving up 13th Street slow down to gawk. Many stop to take photographs or ask questions. Warm Sunday afternoons bring out sightseers.

What was once a three-story rowhouse now stands alone. Houses on either side are long gone. Thompson bought his manor house for $1 and about $2,000 in back taxes. It had been condemned by the city and barricades were keeping pedestrians away from a wall that was already starting to fall.

Not only does Lucky Ray have a single house, he has more land than many Main Liners – a block-long backyard. Behind the house, where an entire block of Camac Street once stood, is nothing but empty space. Thompson bought every lot between Brown and Parrish, fenced it and planted grass.

He plans to install a heart-shaped swimming pool soon. There would be plenty of ground left over for tennis courts – if he played tennis. The squire hosted a church picnic in his backyard for about 50 and had plenty of room for another 50 guests.

Lucky Ray chose the site because he also owns the corner bar a few steps away from his house. An enterprising chap, he also operates a construction/home improvement business. So he already had the labor to get the job done.

A native of the Richmond, Va., area, Lucky Ray missed country living. In some measure he

has brought Virginia to 13th Street with two immense murals painted on his side walls.

One three-story-high painting depicts an actual park he remembers from the South: a Civil War battlefield with a monument, cannon, trees and plenty of blue sky. The wall on the opposite side of the house contains an idyllic rural landscape from Thompson's imagination: a creek, an old mill, trees and a man sitting in the shade.

On the walls not covered by the murals, Thompson has created a fake stone facade. The concrete stones are painted an eye-catching brown and violet. He has also built an enclosed front porch, the roof of which is his second-floor balcony. He also created a picture window in his living room.

The land all around the manor has been landscaped with bushes, trees and flower beds. Crab apple trees were planted on the front sidewalk. In his garden Thompson created two large decorative fountains of his own design. One is star-shaped, and both are illuminated at night by colored lights.

Indoors, Thompson knocked out virtually every interior wall. His second floor may be one of the longest bedrooms in America complete with a sunken bathtub and Jacuzzi.

The squire's living room has a fake fireplace and the same fake-stone look as the exterior. But the walls are painted black and sparkle with silver glitter. One wall is all mirrors and another sports the kind of large landscape often seen in restaurants – ocean waves beating against a rocky coastline.

The 62-year-old Thompson has no master plan: he creates as he goes along. You get the feeling that he'll never complete the job, that he'll always be adding a few fancy touches here and there.

Snobs might feel Lucky Ray's dream house is a bit too gaudy. But it can also be viewed as a

"Lucky Ray" Thompson stands on his balcony.

Mary Alexander at the piano used by cousin John Coltrane to compose music.

symbol of life, hope, renewal – a spark of vitality in a desert of dry bones.

Ray Thompson's House is on the 800 block N. 13th Street. You can't miss it.

JOHN COLTRANE HOUSE

In 1952, the first black family moved into one of the large old houses across from Fairmount Park on 33rd Street in the Strawberry Mansion section.

It wasn't just any family; it was the family of an innovative young jazz performer named John William Coltrane. The musician arrived with his mother, Alice Coltrane; his aunt, Bettie Lyerly; and her daughter, Mary.

The two older women have passed away. Coltrane died in 1967 at age 40 of liver cancer. But Coltrane's cousin, Mary Alexander, remains in the same house. What also remains are numerous items of Coltrane memorabilia and many warm memories of when 1511 N. 33rd was a happy gathering place for jazzmen and their friends.

In 1986 Alexander sought and received historical designation for the house from the Philadelphia Historical Commission. In 1990 a roadside historical marker was placed in front of the house.

Alexander's motivation is partially to honor and perpetuate her cousin's memory, but there is a more important reason for making a shrine out of her own home. The neighborhood had become run-down, plagued with the full array of inner city problems. Alexander, a warm, gregarious retired teacher's aide, thinks she can use Coltrane's legacy as a positive force for neighborhood youth.

She founded an organization called the John W. Coltrane Culture Society and acquired a derelict house adjoining the Coltrane House. The plan is to renovate the property and operate it as a cultural center. It would offer art, music and black awareness programs.

Alexander has launched a few pilot programs in her own backyard. In one instance, two professional drummers provide a lesson in

A piece of jazz by Coltrane.

rhythm to a yard packed with neighborhood pre-schoolers who banged along with the pros on a variety of drums and percussion instruments.

There have also been fund-raising jazz concerts where Alexander managed to squeeze 150 people into her very fruitful and orderly garden.

The Coltrane House is still very much a private residence; but from time-to-time Mary holds an open-house to display Coltrane memorabilia, including record albums, photos, posters, musical scores and notations made by Coltrane and award plaques won by the tenor sax great.

A piano used by Coltrane to compose and arrange on still sits in the same spot. "He lived here from 1952 to 1958 and always came back when he wasn't on the road," says Mary. "He was in and out all of the time and his friends would gather here: Miles Davis, Philly Joe Jones, Shirley Scott, Jimmy Oliver, McCoy Tyner, Jimmy Heath, everybody."

Mary Alexander knew them all and was, herself, very much part of the lively, hip Philly jazz scene of the 1950s and '60s. Coltrane honored her with a blues entitled "Cousin Mary," recorded on his "Giant Steps" album.

The Coltrane House is one of the few homes along 33rd Street that are still well maintained. Inside is a cozy living room furnished with fine old antique chairs and sofas and interesting Art Deco pieces. Two paintings by the jazz giant hang on one wall.

Alexander hopes to aquire more Coltrane items from the musician's two former wives, but the big dream is to get the cultural center next door off and grooving.

The John Coltrane House is at 1511 N. 33rd Street.

A historical marker at the John Coltrane house and the beginnings of a cultural center next door.

MARILYN A. SHAPIRO

Randall School Condominium.

Chapter 21

A TRIO OF FAMOUS
PHILLY APARTMENTS

In any other city an apartment house is just an apartment house, a condominium simply a condo. In Philadelphia where almost everything reeks of history, apartments and condos are no exception.

RANDALL SCHOOL CONDOMINIUM

The first stop on our tour of historic apartments of note is the 900 block of Bainbridge Street. Nestled in the middle of this vintage South Philly block is a three-story brick building that is obviously a former school. In fact, "Randall School" is carved into the building's stonework. If this 19-unit condo had merely been the "Randall School," it would be just another old grammar school, hardly worth a mention.

But the three-story historically certified edifice was a lot more. Before the school district purchased the building in 1903 and turned it into the Randall School, it had been the nationally famous Institute for Colored Youth.

From the late 1840s until about 1900 it was arguably the leading educational facility for blacks in the nation. Its graduates were an honor roll of black leadership of the period.

It was an era when most whites believed blacks were intellectually inferior and even liberal whites saw academic studies above the three R's as a waste of time for black youth.

The school's founding in 1839 by Quakers followed the traditional wisdom. The first location was actually a farm a few miles outside of the city. Its mission was to teach farming, shoemaking "and other useful occupations." Enough money was bequeathed to create a new coeducational high school in 1852 in the heart of the black enclave at 7th and Lombard.

An all-white, Quaker Board of Managers guided the operation, but the principal and faculty were always black. They were bold men and women who dared to create an academic curriculum for blacks which included Latin, Greek, algebra, trigonometry, chemistry, navigation and surveying.

Whites were astounded by the students' abilities to absorb such subjects. For the black community the Institute for Colored Youth was a powerful symbol of hope and pride. Its annual examinations and commencements drew hundreds of black spectators and dozens of whites into overflowing auditoriums to marvel as the scholars performed their stuff.

A new building (the Randall School) opened in 1865 to accommodate students that were now coming from cities all across the country. Public interest was so great that the institute became a tourist attraction, averaging about 30 visitors a week.

The first black teachers in the Philadelphia public schools were products of the Institute. So were the first blacks admitted to the University of Pennsylvania Medical School, Harvard and the Women's Medical College.

Its most beloved faculty member, and a former student, was Octavius V. Catto, murdered during riots in 1871 fomented to prevent blacks from voting.

In its early annual reports the Board of Managers stoutly defended academics for blacks, but reversed their courageous, broad-minded stand during the 1890s. "The teachers should guard against the tendency to devote too much time and attention to studies which lie entirely beyond the future careers of the scholars," the board decreed in 1896. Subjects such as Latin and Greek were dropped. Industrial arts were strengthened.

In 1902 the academic department was closed. The next year the Institute for Colored Youth shut its doors and re-located to the small town of Cheyney in Chester County where farming and the practical skills advocated by Booker T. Washington were the order of the day. The once famous building became just another neighborhood grammar school. But the new farm-school grew to become Cheyney University.

The Randall School (Institute for Colored Youth) is located at 915-925 Bainbridge Street.

CARL MACKLEY APARTMENTS

Our next stop is the blue collar neighborhood of Juniata Park and what until very recently was the Carl Mackley Apartments. New owners have apparently decided the once famous name has lost its luster and have re-christened the complex "Greenway Court."

But it was the Carl Mackley Apartments that excited Franklin D. Roosevelt and his New Deal colleagues. Secretary of Labor Frances Perkins and Secretary of the Interior Harold Ickes both took a personal interest in the project.

When it opened on January 5, 1935, Horatio B. Hackett, director of the Works Progress Administration (WPA), told the assembled crowd, "President Roosevelt has commissioned me to extend to all of you his greetings and congratulations."

The 284-unit complex was the first New Deal public housing project and the first in the nation built by a union with federal financing. It was sponsored by the now defunct Full Fashion Hosiery Works Union, once 10,000 strong in the city. But what really makes the complex historic is its once futuristic design and unheard-of amenities. It was the prototype of today's ubiquitous low-rise, garden apartments.

It was so unusual and innovative that during its first years it attracted a constant stream of visiting government officials, architects, social planners and builders. One visiting architect from the Soviet Union declared it "one of the outstanding housing achievements of the world."

Seen from the street, the Carl Mackley looks something like a fortified medieval city. The rear of the apartments faces the street, creating a monotonous wall of brown and tan building blocks.

Enter the walled-in complex and it's a different story. The apartments look out on pleasant parklike courts. Residents step out onto green

Carl Mackley Apartments.

lawns, flower beds, shrubbery, trees, benches and walkways.

Rents were geared to the average working family's pocket, but the extras were unheard-of elsewhere. There was a swimming pool, hobby shops where menfolk could do carpentry and metalwork and a community auditorium for meetings and parties.

There was a day care center, staffed by capable professionals, where working moms could drop off the kids. This was a unique amenity and was held up as a model during World War II when women were encouraged to join the work force.

It was the first apartment in the city to have a below-ground parking garage. It had rooftop laundry rooms with electric dryers for rainy days – a luxurious novelty in the mid-1930s.

There was a rush of families to rent the new apartments. For years there was a waiting list. An early newspaper article claimed there were 100 names on the list for each of the 284 units.

There was a good deal of idealism in the early years. Tenants started a co-op grocery and established their own credit union. Once in, tenants tended to stay a lifetime. They had a fine, modern apartment and an ideal environment for raising kids, a playground, a club room for older youth with pool tables and ping-pong.

The name honored a 22-year-old union member from Kensington murdered during a long, bitter hosiery mill strike in 1930. Young Carl Mackley and some friends were chasing men filling union jobs, with the idea of roughing up some scabs. One scab worker had a gun and used it against his pursuers. Mackley died and became a union martyr, the kind of working-class hero Woody Guthrie might sing about. The newspapers estimated that 25,000 people attended a public memorial service for Mackley in Kensington.

The complex has changed ownership several times. No one viewing it today would guess it was once the ultimate in "modern living." Its heavy, concrete construction makes it practically fireproof. There's no waiting list these days, but in one aspect it's still in the forefront of change. As Greenway Court, it appears to be the only housing in the neighborhood that is racially integrated.

Greenway Court (Carl Mackley) is bounded by Castor Avenue and M Street, Cayuga and Bristol Streets.

ALDEN PARK

Like the tenants at Carl Mackley Apartments, a lot of residents of the Alden Park Apartments in Germantown wouldn't dream of living anywhere else. But that's where the similarities end. The Mackley was created for blue collar workers. Alden Park was built in the mid-1920s for the Great Gatzby set.

Ask a resident of Alden Park how many rooms are in his apartment, and he'll often stop to count on his fingers. Ten rooms, including quarters for a live-in servant, is not unusual. We're talking large rooms. Often it takes two or three sofas and several chairs to fill a living room. Every apartment has a working fireplace and a dining room with space enough for a real dinner party.

The concept behind Alden Park was to provide the space and luxuries of a large private house without the hassle. The complex is composed of three separate high-rise buildings on a 38-acre site that was once the estate of Justus C. Strawbridge, co-founder of the famous Philadelphia department store Strawbridge & Clothier.

There was enough ground for spacious landscaped gardens, walking paths plus a nine-hole golf course. At some point the golf course was abandoned because too many car windows were being broken.

Gracious living at Alden Park included uniformed doormen, tea parties, a drama group, a paid social planner, a DAR chapter, rental rooms on each floor for guests, chamber music in the lobbies and a swimming pool of Mercer tiles that looks like it's part of a grand European spa.

What's wonderful about Alden Park is that after all these years nothing much has changed. The guest rooms became efficiency apartments during the Depression. But the doormen are still there; so is the drama group, the well-groomed grounds and the posh, old pool. The huge lobbies have been refurnished, grander than ever.

A new owner recently invested millions in the historically certified complex. Some of the city's most prominent names, including Mrs. John B. Kelly, have lived at Alden Park. Many residents of the 700-unit complex have been there for decades. One matron was six months old when she arrived with her parents in 1926. She's still there in the same apartment.

Alden Park Apartments are at Wissahickon and Chelten Avenues.

* * * * *

Alden Park Apartments.

Ancient statues and objects of fine art from many periods grace the Rosenbach Museum & Library.

Chapter 22

NOT YOUR TYPICAL BACHELOR'S PAD

Rosenbach Museum & Library

Which Philadelphia rowhouse contains James Joyce's handwritten manuscript of "Ulysses," George Washington's earliest letter (written at age 17) and Napoleon Bonaparte's personal copy of "The Battle of Marengo"?

Need a few more clues? OK, it's the same rowhouse where Thomas Sully's portrait of Rebecca Gratz hangs in the living room, the silver pitcher of Czar Nicholas I sits in the dining room, and Herman Melville's bookcase stands in a bedroom.

All right, a couple more clues: This rowhouse contains an ancient amulet with King Nebuchadnezzar's name engraved on it and the note Ulysses S. Grant handed to a telegraph operator informing the Secretary of War that Robert E. Lee had just surrendered at Appomattox.

Final clue: The house was owned by two bachelor brothers. One was the world's foremost rare book dealer, the other a renowned dealer in art and antiques.

If you're like most Philadelphians, you still don't know. All right, it's the fabulous Rosenbach Museum & Library.

This is a five-star museum, known by literary scholars and bibliophiles everywhere, yet it remains undiscovered by most natives and rarely gets more than a handful of daily visitors.

You say you're not the type to get goose bumps examining Lewis Carroll's own copy of "Alice in Wonderland" or the oldest handwritten pages (by a medieval scribe) of Chaucer's "Canterbury Tales"? Well, visit the Rosenbach anyway.

For starters, the museum is one of the most handsome 19th century townhouses on one of Philadelphia's classiest blocks. Second, visitors get a tour by excellent guides who make each object interesting.

The museum was the home of Dr. A.S.W. Rosenbach, the premier rare book expert and dealer of his day, and of his older brother, Philip, the antiques maven. The brothers were descendants of Dutch Jews who settled in the city in the early 1800s and had close ties with the famous Gratz family.

The Rosenbach brothers were something like drug dealers with big habits. They kept the best stuff for themselves. They died within a year of each other in the early 1950s, but had set up a foundation and endowment to turn their home into a museum and resource for scholars. They left a ton of great antiques, about 25,000 rare books, and 100,000 manuscripts, letters, illustrations, etc.

The house itself is the only 19th century townhouse (as opposed to mansion) in the city open to the public on a regular basis. In addition to all the fabulous furniture, art and decorative items, the rear garden is certainly among the most charming in Center City.

The rare books and manuscript collection is peerless. The one major drawback is that only

A one-of-a-kind 18th century clock created for French royalty.

The Rosenbach brothers' sitting room is filled with antiques and art.

110

The bookcases seem quite ordinary, but every volume is a rare treasure.

a tiny portion of the literary treasure trove is under glass for public perusal. The only view of most books is through locked glass bookcases. And in most instances the ancient books are contained in fake binders. The public displays are changed often, however.

And the foundation is still collecting new material. For instance, children's author and illustrator Maurice Sendak has donated many of his original drawings to the Rosenbach.

It also acquired the papers and entire contents of the New York apartment of poetess Marianne Moore. One room in the Rosenbach is set up to duplicate her living room. The room shows off Moore's furniture, her trademark cape and tricornered hat, and the baseball memorabilia of a rabid fan.

The book and manuscript collection is incredible. How'd you like to see an original manuscript of Cervantes (the only one in the New World) or chapters of Dickens' "Nicholas Nickleby" in the author's own hand?

One knowledgeable writer called the Rosenbach's "Middle English manuscripts better than Harvard's, Yale's and Princeton's put together. The [Robert] Burns collection is just about the best in the world."

The Rosenbach is particularly rich in the items and manuscripts of Joseph Conrad, Nathaniel Hawthorne, Herman Melville, Emily Dickinson, Charles Dickens, James Joyce, Daniel DeFoe, Lewis Carroll, George Washington, Abraham Lincoln and Benjamin Franklin.

The collection includes original copies of Poor Richard's Almanac and the first book published in America, the 1640 Bay Psalm Book. It has the first map made in America (a 1677 map of New England) and a map of Kentucky drawn with the aid of Daniel Boone.

The Rosenbach owns four sensational photographs of nude little girls taken by Lewis Carroll (he destroyed many others), an original copy of "Pilgrim's Progress," and letters from Mary Queen of Scots.

No, A.W.S. Rosenbach couldn't get Lincoln's copy of the Gettysburg Address. But he obtained the next best thing: the address in which the

the Great Emancipator said "A house divided against itself cannot stand."

Philip Rosenbach's antiques collection includes silver settings from President James Monroe's table, a Philadelphia highboy chest made in 1765 for Michael Gratz, a one-of-a-kind clock made by Marie Antoinette's clockmaker, a large Chippendale dining set, rare oriental rugs, an ornate chest owned by England's Charles II to hold royal papers.

The Rosenbach Museum & Library, 2019 Delancey Place. Tours provided Tuesdays through Sundays from 11 a.m. to 4 p.m. Closed in August and on major holidays. Phone: 732-1600.

✳ ✳ ✳ ✳ ✳

The dining room table is a rare Chippendale; the silver belonged to royalty.

Chapter 23

IT'S A BIRD! IT'S A PLANE!

IT'S EMILIO!

Emilio Carranza Memorial

Trivia bonus question for 50 points: Who was Emilio Carranza and what the heck was he doing in the South Jersey Pine Barrens on the night of July 12, 1928?

Answer: Twenty-three year-old Emilio "The Mexican Lindbergh" Carranza was a long-distance flyer. And on that fateful and stormy night poor Emilio was flying over wooded Tabernacle Township, flashlight in hand, looking for a place to land his failing aircraft.

MARILYN A. SHAPIRO
An eagle plunging to earth symbolizes the fate of Emilio Carranza.

rens, where excitement is rare and therefore memorable.

Many a hiker has been mystified by an odd, rather unimpressive, stone monument in the Pines. It's the Carranza Memorial financed by pennies (centavos?) collected from Mexican school children. A stranger who happens upon the monument on the Saturday closest to July 12 will be more than mystified by the odd assortment of mankind gathered about the memorial: New Jersey State

A daredevil (or simply incompetent) pilot, Carranza had survived 16 crashes during a four-year flying career. He was about to have Crash Number 17, which would be his last.

The fatal crash landing of Emilio was front-page news in both America and Mexico for a day or two. Then the ill-fated aviator was quickly forgotten. But not in the Pine Bar-

Troopers, American Legionnaires, Army brass from Fort Dix, local politicians, folks decked out in full Mexican regalia, a military band, maybe even a mariachi band.

It's Carranza Day in the Pines – an hour of overblown speeches about Mexican-American friendship and syrupy homage to that "gallant airman" who died promoting goodwill between

The Carranza Memorial in the South Jersey pinelands was paid for with pennies collected from Mexican school children.

two great nations. Those who enjoy military pomp, 21-gun salutes, slow motion flag-folding ceremonies will find the annual rites rewarding.

The story behind the Mexican Lindbergh's final flight is an engaging tale with some odd twists. Carranza lived in an era when long-distance flying was the rage. New records were being set constantly. The public was fascinated and enthralled by it all.

Lindbergh captured the world stage with his trans-Atlantic solo flight in May 1927. Carranza, a Mexican Air Force captain, got into the act with non-stop flights from Mexico City to El Paso, Texas, and Mexico City to Los Angeles.

Just six months after Lindbergh's historic flight to Paris, Lucky Lindy flew non-stop from Washington to Mexico City. Another six months passed and the Mexican government

decided to duplicate Lindbergh's flight by sending their own ace from Mexico City to Washington. This was billed as a reciprocal "goodwill" flight.

Carranza left Mexico on June 11, 1928. He flew a Ryan monoplane that was almost a duplicate of Lindbergh's Spirit of St. Louis. He didn't quite make it non-stop to Washington. Fog forced him down in North Carolina. The next day he arrived in the capital to a big welcome. There was a parade, and President Calvin Coolidge welcomed the aviator to the White House.

Carranza spent the next few weeks as guest of honor on the rubber-chicken circuit. In New York, Mayor Jimmy Walker presided over an official welcoming ceremony on the steps of City Hall.

Perhaps all the ceremony was getting on the nerves of this man of action. Impetuously, on July 12, in the middle of a storm, in the middle of the night, Carranza started his return trip to Mexico. Three mechanics at Long Island's Roosevelt Field waved bon voyage. They were the last to see the gallant aviator alive.

The plane crashed in a rather remote area of the woods, known as Sandy Ridge. The body might have gone undiscovered for weeks, but the next day the weather cleared and William H. Carr, 26, of Chatsworth, his wife and his mother drove into the woods to pick wild blueberries. Carr spotted the debris, followed it a short distance, and discovered the body. A short while later, Carr led Burlington County Detective Arthur Carabine and some curiosity seekers to the corpse. The detective found a telegram on the body addressed to Emilio Carranza, which provided the identification. It was a weather report, dated the night before and warning of "cloudy, unsettled" weather.

Canvas from one of the wings was used to wrap the body and it was first taken by car to the small town of Chatsworth, where word quickly spread. A mob of souvenir seekers took to the woods and stripped the scene clean. That night the body lay in a Mount Holly funeral home. Members of the local American Legion Post posted an honor guard.

American Legion Post 11 has ever since made Carranza their special cause. The post conceived the ceremony and has kept it alive all these years. An interesting twist on the Carranza tale evolved as local newspapers retold the Carranza story year-after-year for the annual ceremony.

A 1949 story in the Courier-Post said "Members of the American Legion Post of Mount Holly sent a search party into the wilderness."

Subsquent stories had the hardy legionnaires "hacking through 25 miles of thick brush" to recover the body. Of course there was no search party: no one knew Carranza was missing.

The Mexican government presented $500 checks to Carr and Detective Carabine and elements of mystery and intrigue were added to the Carranza saga. The pair were closely questioned by Mexican officials about the crash site. Yes, there were "rumors" of foul play. Perhaps the plane had been tampered with, the press reported.

A paved road now leads to the stone monument, featuring a carving of a falling eagle and inscriptions in English and Spanish. It sits on state-owned forest land, directly across from public campsites. The scenic Botona Trail passes nearby, making the monument a good place to park and hike.

Probably the strangest thing to happen at the monument was the year Carranza's sister (a pilot) and his widow flew over the site scattering roses from the air. Over the years overly enthusiastic speechmakers have credited Carranza with being "a principal reason for goodwill between the United States and Mexico." One speaker called the spot "sacred" to the people of both nations.

A visiting Mexican college student, whose American host thought the visitor would really enjoy the event, attended the 1990 ceremony. Asked if he had ever heard of the gallant Carranza, the Mexican student raised his eyes and shrugged his shoulders, an international gesture of bewilderment meaning "Who?"

The Carranza Monument is near the dead end of Carranza Road, which intersects with Route 206 near the Red Lion Circle in Burlington County, N.J.

✴ ✴ ✴ ✴ ✴

*Solidly built houses were rented to Roebling workers
and later sold to them at bargain prices.*

Chapter 24

ROMANIAN (AND HUNGARIAN)
SPOKEN HERE
Roebling, New Jersey

It certainly doesn't fall into the category of "tourist attraction," but there's no other town in the region quite like Roebling, N.J. Its history is unique. Its look and feel are different from any other place in the area.

The special flavor comes, in part, from its isolation. Situated on the Delaware River between Burlington and Trenton, Roebling has only one road leading directly into it. The town lies unseen just off Route 130: No one passes through by chance.

Roebling suddenly sprang nearly full-blown, out of empty farmland in 1905. It was the quintessential "company town" with 4,000 residents, all employees of the John A. Roebling steel plant and their dependents.

With business booming at the firm's Trenton mill and no room to expand there, the firm built a huge steel mill and related buildings on farmland 12 miles south of Trenton.

It also built an entirely self-sufficient town around the plant. Then it assembled a labor force: Americans and Swedes for supervisory and skilled positions, and hundreds of recently arrived strong-armed immigrants from Central Europe: Romanians, Hungarians, Slovaks and Russians.

Large Victorian homes were built close to the river for supervisors. More than 700 rental brick rowhouses went up for married workers and their families. Large boarding houses were constructed for single men.

A nearly block-long company store provided everything from potatoes to the stove to cook them on. Prices were low and credit available. The Roebling Inn was a sprawling beer hall, with bowling lanes in the cellar. The company created a park with a bandstand, ball fields, family garden plots, an auditorium for live shows and boxing. Later, movies were shown seven days a week. There was a boathouse, post office, fire company, a school.

Just across the railroad tracks on non-company land, small shops, bars, butchers and bakeries sprang up to service the town. Here, too, the immigrants built their churches and social clubs: two Romanian churches, two Hungarian churches, a Slavic orthodox church. The

Hungarian Club closed, but the Sfante Maria Roumanian Society and the American-Slovak Club are still active.

On June, 30, 1974, the plant locked its gates for good. Yet everything else remains unchanged. The former steelworkers and their sons still live in the same neat rowhouses, generation succeeding generation. It's a company town without the company. It takes only the slightest imagination to hear the mill's whistles signal a change of shifts and to see, in the mind's eye, platoons of lunch pail-toting steelworkers marching down to Number One Gate.

By all accounts, Roebling Steel was a special place to work. Few industrial work forces were more contented, proud or loyal to the company than the men and women of Roebling.

John Roebling was the famous developer of steel cables and builder of the Brooklyn Bridge, a project that cost his life. His sons, Ferdinand, Charles, and Civil War veteran Colonel Washington Roebling built a company of international stature. The men and women of

Retired Roebling steelworkers pose proudly with a cross-section of cable made for the Golden Gate Bridge.

Roebling produced everything from the cables of the Golden Gate Bridge to hair-thin wire for watchmakers.

The family was a model of enlightened paternalism. In the depths of the 1930s Depression, hours were cut but no workers were laid off. No one was evicted from company-owned houses. Rents were simply postponed for years. No utilities were shut off; no one was allowed to go hungry.

The sprawling steel mill complex is now quietly rusting.

"My rent was $8 a month when I moved into this house in 1936 and only $13 in 1947, when the Roeblings sold all the houses to the workers," recalls retired steelworker John Borbi. "They charged $3,800 for the house; a real bargain."

A long feature story on the company town in a 1924 edition of Iron Age Magazine concludes with a question: Is the expense of operating a company town worth it? "Not in dollars and cents . . . in the last analysis there is distinct loss measured in money. But it most assuredly does pay in the larger sense . . . in promoting permanence of employment and hence in costly labor turnover." And, concludes the magazine, it pays off in assimilation of the "foreign element, which forms so large a share of what we have become accustomed to call common labor."

The Roebling family sold the plant in 1953 to Colorado Fuel & Iron, which kept the mill going for another 20 years.

The memories are very much alive for the thousands who have never known another home, and perhaps, another job. The former union hall is now a library. But there's a room where retirees play cards and wile away time. Another room has been set aside as a museum filled with mementos, old photos and products of the mill.

There's an active Roebling Historical Society, which publishes "The Roebling Record, a Pastiche of Pride, Performance, Pre-Eminence & Perservance." A nostalgic article recalls the day in 1930 when the local semiprofessional Roebling Blue Centers played the first-ever professional indoor football game in Atlantic City's Convention Hall. Another article recalls three days of bloody fistfighting between Hungarian and Romanian workers.

The entire town has been placed on the National Register of Historical Places and the steel mill has been placed on the Superfund Clean-up list. Almost everything is still there. Unfortunately the "Pest House" where residents considered "pests," such as belligerent drunks, were exiled until their behavior improved, is gone.

Probably the best time to visit the town is during ethnic fairs held at St. Nicholas Byzantine Church. The historical society has put out a comprehensive brochure on the town with a map of its landmarks.

Roebling is in Florence Township in Burlington County. To get there take Route 130 North. About a mile past the Pennsylvania/New Jersey Turnpike Bridge is a sign for the left-turn leading to Roebling.

An Orthodox church serves the spiritual needs of immigrant Eastern European workers.

The old union hall now contains a museum recalling Roebling's history.

Chapter 25

A NICE, RESPECTABLE
SUBURBAN COMMUNE
Bryn Gweled

In the long, often bizarre saga of utopian living schemes and experiments embraced by idealists, Bryn Gweled Homesteads in lower Bucks County stands out as unique.

Why? Because it actually worked. Try to find anyone at home at Brook Farm or New Harmony. Find just one living, breathing hippie commune.

By contrast, Bryn Gweled celebrated its 50th anniversary in 1990 and chances are it will be there for a 100th-birthday bash. Here is a community of idealists who, for once, had their heads screwed on right.

The idea was born in Bedford House, a South Philadelphia settlement house at 6th and Kater, during the bleak Depression years. Its director, Herbert Bergstrom, was interested in the ideas of a now forgotten dreamer, Ralph Borsodi, who started a cooperative living experiment in

Sign of a unique community.

Suffern, N.Y. These folks not only tried to grow their own food, they also raised sheep so they could make their own wool sweaters.

Bergstrom and other settlement house workers visited the commune. They talked long and thought deeply about the principles and practicality of cooperative living, then gathered like-minded utopians and in late 1938 began planning the future. The group located a 232-acre rural site in Upper Southampton Township with a price tag of $18,000. A hat was passed; everyone put an unsigned slip in stating how much money he could immediately raise. "When the hat came back, the total was $20,000," Bergstrom later recalled.

The principles of these clear-eyed dreamers were simple. First, there was a commitment to racial and religious diversity. Today there are

Bryn Gweled veterans Judy Osterman and Ed Potts proudly survey the new community hall.

several black families, assorted Jews, Catholics, Quakers, atheists, young couples, old fogies, white collars and blue collars.

Members decided to keep their city jobs, but they would try various cooperative buying schemes. Land would be owned jointly, but members would build and own their houses.

They were ecologists decades before the word existed. Eighty acres of streams and woods would forever remain untouched. The community battled with the utility companies to have telephone and electric lines buried underground and eventually dug the trenches themselves. Houses were built on wooded two-acre lots. No fences and no sidewalks.

Together the homesteaders built and maintain a community center, swimming pool, soccer field, ice skating pond and all internal roads. By the end of World War II, 14 families had established homes, and over the next cou-

ple of decades the community expanded to its limit of 75 houses.

A family that wants to join the community – when a member moves or dies – is first interviewed by a committee where the ideas of Bryn Gweled are laid out. The candidate then meets every family, usually over dinner, and attends the monthly meetings. The process takes a minimum of six months. It then requires a four-fifths majority to vote in a new family. At this writing, 12 families have gone through the process and are waiting for an opening.

It's not everybody's cup of tea and some candidates drop out. Bryn Gweled folk are big on committees – practically everyone is on a committee or two. Monthly meetings can become long, and debate passionate. Residents are expected to participate in weekend work parties – clearing brush, draining the pond, fixing the plumbing in the community center.

The rewards for all this work and commitment come in being part of a genuine, caring community. You're not alone. Sick in bed? Can't cook or take care of the kids? Not to worry. Volunteer baby-sitters and casseroles are on the way. You may not be buddy–buddy with all 75 families, but you certainly know everyone's name and telephone number.

In the old days there was a food co-op that folded. Only a few years ago, cooperative buying of heating oil and gasoline ceased because the community could no longer find a good deal.

Perhaps the most impressive aspect of Bryn Gweled is the physical beauty and charm of the place. It's only about a mile north of the busy intersection of Street Road and Bustleton Pike in Feasterville. Just about all the surrounding farms and open land have filled up with tract housing. But Bryn Gweled, with its buffer of woods, still seems separate and distant from the suburban sprawl. There's a strong feeling – or simply an illusion – of country living.

It's worth a visit just to eyeball the houses. A few nonconformists built colonial-style homes, but the vast majority are the one-story, ultra-modern variety of the Frank Lloyd Wright-school, with huge picture windows, a lot of glass walls and natural woods. They fit snuggly and naturally into the landscape. It's undeniably a handsome community.

In the early days, gawking Sunday drivers were common. Veteran homesteader Edward Potts says his wife once gazed from their wide picture window and was startled to find an entire class of architectural students from the University of Pennsylvania looking back.

To go to Bryn Gweled take Street Road (Route 132) north. Make right onto Gravel Hill Road then make first right.

✳ ✳ ✳ ✳ ✳

The Plotnicks, Ashley, Debbie, Max, Alex and Michael, love their house with its glass front and woodsy setting.

CIGNA owns this famous portrait of Ben Franklin painted in 1850, long after his death.

Chapter 26

THE WONDERFUL WORLD
OF FIRE MARKS
CIGNA Museum

Do you like model ships? Do you get a thrill out of old fire engines? Do you enjoy paying your insurance bills?

If your answer is yes to any or all of the above questions, you'll want to visit CIGNA insurance company headquarters in Center City. You don't have to pay premiums to this giant insurance firm to drop by the CIGNA Museum, a quality collection of art and artifacts in what seem to be the unrelated subjects of fire-fighting and ships.

There is a link between fire hoses and anchor chains at CIGNA. The firm was founded in Philadelphia in 1792 as the Insurance Company of North America (INA), to insure ship cargoes and write fire insurance. During two centuries the company accumulated a lot of material on ships and fire-fighting.

It created a museum in the early 1920s, making it one of the oldest corporate museums in the nation, and one of the best with about 9,000 items. Many objects are displayed in company offices here and abroad or are on loan to other institutions. But some of the most significant pieces can be seen at the company museum.

For years, the museum was in the block-long CIGNA building at 16th and Arch. While the vintage fire engines and giant ship models remain in the lobby on Arch Street, the museum has relocated just a few blocks away to Two Liberty Place.

The museum's strength is in fire-fighting, and the true fire-buff will find a visit rewarding. Just for starters, CIGNA has the world's largest collection of fire marks – those plaques affixed to 18th and 19th century houses by fire insurance companies. Contrary to popular myth, American insurance companies did not pay firemen to fight fires on properties that displayed their fire mark. The mark was really an advertising device.

There is a rich and colorful tradition of fire-fighting in Philadelphia. In an era without television or professional sports, fire-fighting became an all-consuming social activity, a competitive outlet, an avenue of male-bonding, community solidarity, and a base of political power. The rivalry among companies was so bitter that it led to cutting hoses, gunfights,

Vintage pumpers in the CIGNA collection.

even to setting false alarms to lay an ambush. The bloodshed and lawlessness of some companies were a major reason volunteer companies were abolished in 1871 and a professional department funded.

The more civilized competition among volunteer companies is well-illustrated in the CIGNA collection. There are paintings and prints depicting fire engine races and a famed Philadelphia competition to determine which company's hoses could squirt a higher stream of water into the air.

The volunteers seemed to outstrip Masonic lodges when it came to colorful regalia and decorative arts. The collection is rich in this folk art, such as decorative panels placed on fire engines for parades. There are displays of badges, banners and wide leather belts decorated with company insignia. There are also exhibits of highly decorated fire helmets, en-

graved speaking trumpets, torches and artfully decorated leather fire buckets.

The museum displays a full array of the tools of the trade: wrenches and spanners, hooks, axes, hoses, wooden hydrants, primitive fire extinguishers, sections of wood pipes and the loud rattles used to rouse residents in case of fire.

CIGNA has a huge art collection and among its fire-fighting paintings is the famous portrait of Benjamin Franklin wearing a fire helmet, headgear that was unknown at the time. Another memorable canvas, nearly six feet high, is an action-filled depiction of a horse-drawn engine racing to a fire scene.

The museum also displays seascapes and paintings of sailing ships, plus items and documents associated with the company's history. Included is a large silver trophy cup presented to a British captain whose vessel rescued an American ship in distress in the Persian Gulf in

1807. INA had $35,000 in insurance money (a huge sum then) at risk and was super-grateful to the rescue ship.

The most valuable and impressive items in the collection are certainly the manual and horse-drawn pumpers, engines and other apparatus on display in the lobby at 16th to 17th and Arch Street. A piece called "The Pioneer" is America's oldest existing steam fire engine, built in 1857. There is a hand pumper built in Philadelphia in 1792 and another dating to 1841. There is also a perfectly preserved, horse-drawn hook and ladder from the 1890s.

CIGNA has an entire staff of curators and archivists. Among the items in their care are thousands of blueprints of old Philadelphia houses. These plans were needed to obtain the company's perpetual fire insurance – a policy that could be passed on to new owners. In fact, about 6,000 of these old INA policies are still in effect.

CIGNA Museum is at Two Liberty Place, 1601 Chestnut Street, seventh floor. Fire engines are on Arch Street between 16th and 17th. Best to call ahead. Phone: 761-4909

✳ ✳ ✳ ✳ ✳

A small sample of the world's largest collection of fire marks.

Equipment to thrill any fire-buff.

Chapter 27

NO, IT'S NOT A
NEW GREEK RESTAURANT
The Athenaeum

You're not likely to visit another private Philadelphia institution with the elegance and classic clubbiness of this perfectly preserved 19th century temple of the rich and studious.

Why? Because no similar sanctuary of the old aristocracy is likely to open its doors to some peon with mustard stains on his T-shirt. Try walking into the Rittenhouse Club or the Union League some day "just to look around."

Most folks would never think of entering this classic gem on Washington Square, either. "It is intimidating," admits its pleasant, unintimidating director, Roger Moss. Yet anyone who rings the front doorbell is welcome to come inside and gawk to his heart's content.

And the Athenaeum is now completing changes to ameliorate that intimidating chill. Glass doors will be added to the entrance, and most of the first floor will become exhibit space to show off its many treasures.

The most impressive sights, however, are the grand reading room, chess room and meeting room on the second floor. The visitor has only to request permission to ascend the stairs, and it is granted.

Founded in 1814, as a private subscription library, the society takes its name from Athena, the Greek godess of wisdom. This was a popular moniker at the time, but there is no connection with the Boston Athenaeum or like-named institutions in other cities.

The bibliophiles first utilized Ben Franklin's Philosophical Society for library space. In the late 1830s the library sponsored a design contest for a building of its own. Practically every major architect of the era submitted plans. The winner was John Notman. His rather austere design became the first Italian Renaissance Revival-style building in the city and one of its first brownstones. Its classic lines have often been copied.

Ironically, this architectural jewel, completed in 1845, is built on the site of the former Walnut Street Prison. Archaeological exploration in the Athenaeum's walled garden yielded 7,000 intriguing artifacts of the prison, including homemade dice.

The most elegant and impressive space in the building is the members' reading room with its tall glass bookcases, floor-to-ceiling windows and wood pillars supporting a 24-foot-high ceiling. A stately grandfather's clock is the only sound to penetrate the stately dignity. Each day a cut-glass decanter of sherry is place on a reading table for members who may wish to sip a bit with their reading. How's that for class?

Even the water cooler is a peerless antique dating to 1873, and the large world globe was made in London in 1894. There are 100,000 volumes and some very specialized collections donated by members: collections on Sherlock Holmes, railroading and a 200-book section on fox hunting.

More impressive than the books is the priceless collection of antiques and art donated or purchased over the decades. "Wherever you look, treasures meet the eye," declares an early guidebook.

Surprising treasures that somehow found their way to the Athenaeum are a death mask

The dignified elegance of the members' reading room at the Athenaeum.

of Napoleon Bonaparte and the magnificent "escutcheon," or oramental plaque, that decorated the carriage Napoleon took to his coronation in Notre Dame Cathedral in 1804.

The organization seemed to have a particular affection for French art and furniture. Several rare pieces came from the Bordentown, N.J., estate of Joseph Bonaparte (brother of Napoleon and former King of Spain). The walls are heavy with paintings and portraits by 18th and 19th century artists, including works by Emanuel Leutze and John Neagle.

There are about 1,300 Athenaeum shareholders. Membership is often passed from one generation to the next, like a family heirloom. As time passed the Athenaeum tottered along bereft of any real purpose. The old families supported the place because it was beautiful and historic. But who the heck really needed a private library in the 20th century?

Now, new directions have revitalized the staid edifice and the place buzzes with vigor as it concentrates all its efforts into architecture, design and furnishings.

Among its early members were some of the city's, and the nation's, top architects. The city that spawned "the Philadelphia Lawyer" also produced many of the nation's greatest architects. The Athenaeum became the repository of a sizable collection of important architectural drawings. And from 1847 to 1870 the local chapter of the American Institute of Architects had offices in the Athenaeum.

Sometime in the 1970s, it decided to concentrate all its energies into early American architecture and design. In a short time, the collection has grown from about 15,000 architectural drawings to 130,000.

Original drawings include the Capitol Building in Washington, Girard College, Benjamin Franklin Bridge, Moyamensing Prison and the

Wall-to-ceiling windows light the reading room.

earliest drawings of Independence Hall. There are thousands of banks, churches, schools, Victorian mansions.

It has also accumulated perhaps America's most extensive collection of 19th century and Victorian-era interior design materials: wallpaper sample books, paint cards, furniture catalogues, samples of wood trim and moldings.

Owners of very old houses often seek help at the Athenaeum and sometimes find the original plans and drawings of their homes.

Its resources are listed in two nationwide computer networks and it gets thousands of requests each year for information.

The Athenaeum, 219 S. 6th Street. Open to visitors Mondays through Fridays, 9 a.m. to 5 p.m. Researchers should make a prior appointment. Phone: 925-2688

✳ ✳ ✳ ✳ ✳

A new and unique Philadelphia institution, the Balch Institute.

Chapter 28

IN PRAISE OF THE MELTING POT
Balch Institute

When upper-crust Philadelphian Emily Swift Balch died in 1917, she left about $1 million for any grandchildren her two sons might father. If the sons died without progeny, the will directed the money go to build a library. Both sons died in 1927 without children, and for nearly 50 years there was no library.

The money lay in a trust fund building interest until some organizations in the 1960s learned there was a windfall waiting to be spent. By this time the account had grown to $8 million.

The matter was left to the wisdom of Orphans Court Judge Charles Klein. It took Klein 10 years to untangle legal complications and decide how to spend the Balch funds, which now stood at $10 million.

Balch's will left no guidelines for the library, so Klein called for suggestions. There were plenty of proposals, but the idea that captured the judge's fancy just might have poor Emily Swift Balch spinning in her grave. The cash for the grandkids who never came

has financed an immigration–ethnic studies library and museum: a place to honor and record the trials and triumphs of immigrant coal miners from Poland, Jewish peddlers and Irish barkeepers.

You see, Mrs. Balch's Anglo-Saxon forebears arrived in Maryland in 1658, even before William Penn sailed up the Delaware.

The Balch Institute of Ethnic Studies opened for business in a modern $5 million building in 1976. It has already earned a niche among Philadelphia's outstanding cultural and educational institutions and is rapidly acquiring a worldwide reputation.

Its unique mission should interest all those whose ancestors did not arrive aboard the Mayflower. It is trying to fill a big void. Ethnicity, among many groups, is fading quickly, while the saga of immigration and absorption continues with little formal documentation.

Balch wants to save it all: every yellowing Yiddish newspaper, every Slovak wedding dress, every annual report of the Ancient Order of Hibernians. It seeks to document the folkways of the newer immigrant groups from Asia and Latin America before they, too, disappear into the melting pot.

Starting from zero, the Balch Library now has 60,000 books and a growing archive containing thousands of photos, periodicals, letters, diaries, memoirs and miscellaneous objects ranging from ship ticket stubs to ethnic sheet music.

In fact, Balch can already claim preeminence in the field. Only the University of Minnesota has a similar library collection that encompasses every ethnic group. While the library and documents exist mostly for scholars and those interested in genealogy, Judge Klein wanted something more lively than another stuffy library for bookworms. This goal is carried out through the Institute's museum and its many social and educational activities.

The museum area is not large, but the changing displays and video presentations are well-done and interesting. More important is a full schedule of lectures, symposiums, ethnic entertainment, music, films, and bus tours of ethnic neighborhoods and restaurants.

Balch also provides space for the independent Philadelphia Jewish Archive Center. But the most fascinating activity in the building takes place behind closed doors in the basement where clerks sit at computer terminals, slowly completing a task of giant proportions.

They are laboring on a joint Balch/Temple University project to computerize the names of 25 to 30 million immigrants who entered the United States between 1820 and 1924: the ancestors of about half of all Americans now living.

The father of the project is Temple economics professor Dr. Ira Glazier, who volunteered to help solve a space problem for the National Archives in Washington by taking 11 tons of paper off their hands. He carted off the mani-

fests (passenger lists) of every immigrant ship that docked in America for 100 years. The government required captains to turn over the names, nationalities, ages, sex, occupations and other data about all passengers.

Back in the 1940s these historic lists were microfilmed. The old manifests – mostly handwritten – were taking up valuable space until Glazier and Temple took them. The expense, and the enormity of the work required to computerize such a mass of data, has far exceeded expectations. After nearly a decade of effort, only 15 percent of the lists have been processed.

Financing has come from various sources; the most important have been private publishing houses specializing in genealogy. The first project completed was computerizing

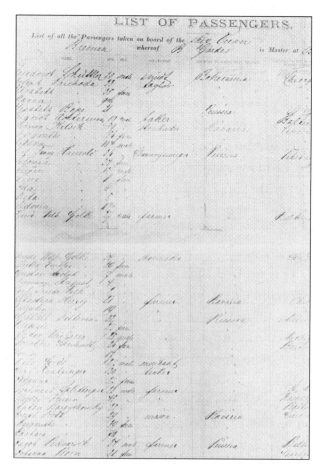

Thousands of immigrant ship passenger lists are being computerized at Balch.

A Balch Institute display on the ethnic press in America.

the names of the 700,000 Irish immigrants who arrived during the potato famine years of 1840-1851. The publisher who financed the work used the computer tapes to print a seven-volume set of books.

For several years the computer clerks have been punching in the names of four million German immigrants who arrived since 1840. Again, a publisher has provided most of the cash, but the German government has also contributed. A new project involving Italian immigration is starting.

The work is certainly important for historians. But it should also be exciting to millions of average Americans who will eventually be able to type the name of an ancestor into a computer and instantly learn the day he arrived in America plus many other facts about the newcomer.

The Balch Institute, 18 S. 7th Street, (below Market Street). Open Mondays through Saturdays, 10 a.m. to 4 p.m. Phone: 925-8090

＊ ＊ ＊ ＊ ＊

A bust of Henry George.

Chapter 29

A CABAL OF DEDICATED GEORGISTS
Henry George School

There's something fascinating and admirable about dedication to a cause, philosophy or hero that everyone else in the world seems to have forgotten decades ago.

Does the name "Henry George" ring a bell? Perhaps a very faint tinkle? Somewhere in your old textbook for American History 101, there was a paragraph about Henry George. In the 30-year-old history book on the author's shelf, it's a long paragraph in the chapter headed Radical Reformers: "In 1879 Henry George, a California newspaperman published 'Progress and Poverty,' a forthright attack on the maldistribution of wealth in the United States..."

Actually, the book was a hell of a best-seller that was printed in 25 languages and eventually sold many millions of copies.

There's plenty of Georgist reading matter.

George's one big idea was the land tax or "single tax." Tax land rather than structures, said George. This would end land speculation, stimulate development and eliminate the need for all other taxes.

A lot of deep thinkers ranging from Leo Tolstoy to Albert Einstein have praised George and his socioeconomic ideas. "Single Tax" clubs formed around the nation to push the idea. A handful of governmental units have put the land tax idea into practice in modified form. The city of Pittsburgh is one.

George ran twice for mayor of New York and died just before the election of 1897. Although his appeal was mainly to populists, apparently a few moneyed folks were also followers. In 1932 they opened a free school in New York City to teach Georgian theory and economics.

In fact, they had enough money to open and support 13 Henry George Schools, including a branch that opened in Philadelphia in 1935.

Unlike the other 12 locations, which are simply buildings of no special importance, the Philadelphia branch is a historic shrine dear to the hearts of all George-followers. It's Henry's birthplace.

Yes, the old radical was born in a modest brick rowhouse on 10th Street near Lombard. Pop sold religious books for a living. The family didn't stay long. Shortly after Henry's birth they moved to a house on Third Street near Queen. But the house on 10th Street is very old and quaint, and its connection to Henry George adds extra relevancy to the school.

A bedroom has been set up as a museum to duplicate the room where George was born. In fact, its main feature is the very bed on which the self-educated economist was born. It was donated to the school by George's granddaughter, famed dancer Agnes DeMille.

Courses are held in the evening and carry no credit. The only charge is a modest fee for books and registration and the classes are open to anyone. The teachers are unpaid volunteers from various walks of life. In most cases, they took all the courses, got hooked on George and stayed to teach.

Despite the bargain tuition, the basic Georgian study classes don't attract very large crowds; three to six students per 10-week session seems to be the norm. A course entitled "How Wall Street Works" attracts larger numbers. There are also a series of Saturday afternoon seminars on economic and social topics.

The school does have a paid director. The man currently holding that post is Mike Curtis, a former tree-trimmer with Georgian links in his own family tree. He says his grand-

A historical marker points out the birthplace of Henry George.

father joined a cadre of Henry George Single Tax advocates who descended upon the state of Delaware in 1895. They believed they had a chance of winning one small state over to the cause, but got only three percent of the vote.

In 1900, however, George followers founded the town of Arden, Del. – the director's home town – and put into effect the land tax, which is still in force. The land is owned by the community and homeowners pay an annual rent, in lieu of property taxes.

While not wild-eyed fanatics who expect Georgian economics to sweep the nation soon, Curtis and the staff stoutly maintain that George's principles are valid and could help alleviate a host of problems, including the rehabilitation of slum neighborhoods.

A scene inside the Henry George School.

Visitors are always welcome to brouse, discuss economics or pick up literature. Yes, there are free copies available of two Georgist newspapers to take home and ponder.

The Henry George School is at 413 S. 10th Street. Phone: 922-4278

＊ ＊ ＊ ＊ ＊

Of course there's a statue of William Penn at Pennsbury Manor.

Chapter 30

A NICE SUBURBAN HOUSE, CLOSE TO THE TURNPIKE
Pennsbury Manor

Of course, Philadelphia is fine for the laboring classes and petty bourgeoisie, packed like sardines into their little brick townhouses. But people of quality require spacious quarters, green vistas and plenty of room for servants.

So, as William Penn was penciling the street grid and public squares for his City of Brotherly Love, he was also sketching details for a plush baronial estate for himself – 27 miles up river from the urban riffraff.

The 8,400-acre spread was a kind of Quaker State "Tara" with orchards, fields, barns, numerous outbuildings, formal gardens, servants galore and a two-story (plus attic) Georgian-style brick manor house on the crystal clear Delaware River.

Pennsbury Manor in Bucks County turned out as impressive and handsome as the proprietor of Pennsylvania had planned. But its history is a rather melancholy tale. Penn had little opportunity to play the role of country squire. The place was probably incomplete during his first brief stay in the colony, from July 1682 to fall 1684.

He returned from England in 1699, spent the spring and summer of 1700 at Pennsbury with his wife Hannah, daughter Letitia, and infant son, John. Once more legal hassles forced Penn to return to England with the family in 1701.

Employees ran the plantation, and Penn wrote a lot of letters about how things should be done (he was particularly interested in the garden) — but he never returned. He died and was buried in England in 1718.

When Penn's son Thomas visited Pennsbury in 1736, he found the place in an advanced stage of decay. Grandson Richard Penn was going to restore the shambles in 1775, when war broke out. Richard, being a Loyalist, fled to England. There was little left by 1800. A farmer named Crozier purchased the land and built his house over the foundation of Penn's manor house.

What exists today is a re-creation of the grand estate financed by federal money in the 1930s and administered by the Pennsylvania Historical and Museum Commission.

With hundreds of 18th and even 17th century houses and estates still standing in and around

A guide at Pennsbury Manor in full Colonial costume.

the city, why would anyone want to visit a 50-year-old re-creation?

Because they've done a terrific job. Researchers and architects took great pains to get it right, make it authentic. And it's a beautiful spot and a terrific destination for a family outing – it's educational and fun. Pack a picnic lunch and spend the day.

There's a lot to see and well-informed, enthusiastic guides in Colonial costume to make it come alive. The visit begins with an informative slide show, followed by a guided tour lasting an hour or more.

What makes Pennsbury particularly appealing to kids is the livestock. Geese, guinea fowl, chickens, turkeys and peacocks roam the place. There are sheep, cattle, horses and a donkey.

Outbuildings include an icehouse, smokehouse, stable, blacksmith shop and joiner's (carpenter's) shop. The original bake and brew house stood into the middle of the 19th century, and the re-creation is quite authentic. The oven

is large enough to bake 30 loaves of bread at one shot, and from time to time a batch of bread is baked.

In fact, there's a regular schedule of "Living History" events and demonstrations: blacksmithing, woodworking, open hearth cooking, gardening workshops and some recent experiments in beer making. There are "living theater" days and a festive candlelight Christmas program.

The manor is built on the original foundations and furnished with authentic 17th century antiques. Only one large pewter serving platter actually belonged to Penn. It was given as a wedding present to two servants and remained in that family for generations.

The 43-acre site is in a particularly isolated and scenic spot. An untouched, wooded island in the Delaware River screens New Jersey, so the view is probably much the way it appeared to Penn. The orchards, vineyard and gardens are particularly pretty.

Pennsbury is a bit off the beaten track, about five miles north of Bristol. However, that final stretch is, in itself, interesting. What appear to be large bays or lakes are actually old sand and gravel quarries that filled with water. The motorist also passes what must be one of the world's largest trash landfills, an interesting and aromatic attraction.

Pennsbury Manor is open Tuesdays through Saturdays from 9 a.m. to 5 p.m.; Sundays, noon to 5 p.m. Tours are offered year-round. Call ahead for the schedule of special programs. Pennsbury can be reached by either I-95 or the Pennsylvania Turnpike to Route 13. Follow the direction signs at Green Lane and Route 13 to Radcliffe Street. Phone: 946-0400

✳ ✳ ✳ ✳ ✳

The manor provided an opulent home for the founder of Pennsylvania.

Among the items of theater memorabilia at the Charlotte Cushman Club
is a crown worn by Sarah Bernhardt.

Chapter 31

THE ROAR OF THE GREASEPAINT
Charlotte Cushman Club

It started in 1907 when a press agent's gimmick and 19 chorus girls motivated a compassionate society matron to launch what has become a venerable but little-known Philadelphia institution.

It's the Charlotte Cushman Club founded as a safe, respectable and reasonably priced residence for visiting actresses. Today an occasional theater person – male or female – rents one of the club's three bedrooms during a Philadelphia run. It also provides a cozy and inspirational atmosphere for visiting show biz people to relax, read or study lines.

But mostly it's a gathering place for local theater lovers. Members throw a gala cast party whenever new plays come to town and present an annual theater award that has become quite prestigious.

For visitors, the Charlotte Cushman Club is an opportunity to bask in the city's best collection of nostalgic theater memorabilia and to enjoy a very charming place.

The history of the club begins with a feature story that appeared on April 16, 1907 in the defunct North American headlined "Chorus Girls Establish Communist Boarding House in the City, Where They Live in Royal Style."

In words and photos the story claimed chorus girls of a visiting show, "The Snow Man," had jammed into a rented house on Spring Garden Street where they pooled resources and shared chores. The show girls just couldn't afford a decent hotel or boardinghouse on their meager pay.

Mrs. George Spencer Morris read the story and wrote a note inviting the girls to her house for tea. With a push from press agent George H. Atkinson, five ladies of the chorus accepted the invitation and heard Mrs. Morris discuss the need for a respectable lodging for theater women.

Within the year, the energetic Mrs. Morris had raised the funds and founded the club named in honor of America's leading actress of the 19th century, Boston-born Charlotte Cushman (1813-1876)

More than 40 years later, press agent Atkinson fessed up. The "commune" of chorus girls was faked. He had repeated a stunt first hatched in Boston. The house on Spring Garden Street was rented for only one day. He knew the press would gobble up the story, lured by the photo opportunities.

In fact, there was a real need for such a residency and Mrs. Morris had pondered the possibility even before the phony newspaper story.

The club moved several times. In 1929, local news gal Laura Lee reported on her visit to the club, then at 1010 Spruce Street. "There are 50 girls in the house, I was told, and often there are 100 on the waiting list. . . . The club has given girls of the theater . . . a happy, peaceful home while on the road, with meals that mother used to make."

Among the young actresses who used the club were Helen Mencken and Helen Hayes. Many famous theater people of the 1920s and '30s visited and donated furnishings.

During the Depression and war years the club closed its living facilities and rented hotel suites. After the war it located at 1216 Locust, and in the mid-1960s the club moved to its present locale on quaint, narrow Camac Street. The building dates to the 1850s and had formerly served as the all-male Yachtsman Club.

It's a fascinating place, filled with photos and paintings of theater greats of the past. There are display cases filled with rare 19th century theater artifacts: a crown worn by Sarah Bernhardt in "Medea," a very old make-up kit, locks of hair from the beautiful Fanny Kemble, oil-burning stage footlights, theater jewelry and costumes.

There are historic portraits of Cushman, Edwin Forrest, Junius Brutus Booth, Joseph Jefferson, Bernhardt and many 19th century theater bills.

The Charlotte Cushman Club
on scenic Camac Street.

Many items have stories attached. Henry Fonda and Andy Gibb are remembered for tinkling the ivories of the baby grand piano donated by Fanny Brice. The fireplace equipment was donated by George Arliss. And Jose Ferrer is remembered for taking over the basement lounge and giving daily acting lessons.

The club also has a terrific collection of books, plays, old playbills and theater magazines stretching back to the turn of the century.

Some of the biggest names in show business have come to the club to accept the annual Charlotte Cushman Award launched in 1957. The list includes Mary Martin, Katharine Hepburn, Richard Burton, Peter Ustinov, Helen Hayes, Joshua Logan, Jose Ferrer, Shirley Booth and Carol Channing.

The club has an extensive collection of books on the theater and old scripts.

The club limits its membership because of the limited size of the house. Christmas and opening night parties are often memorable events that swing until the wee hours. The full-time club director will show visitors around, but call for an appointment first.

The Charlotte Cushman Club is at 239 S. Camac Street. Call first. Phone: 735-4676.

✳ ✳ ✳ ✳ ✳

An ornate cupola tops the Ryerss Mansion.

Chapter 32

A TRIP TO THE EXOTIC EAST
IN THE FAR NORTHEAST
Robert W. Ryerss Mansion

Many Philadelphians will tell you that aside from discount department stores and bowling alleys, there ain't much culture in the vast Northeast section of the city.

That's not entirely true. There's the Ryerss Mansion, a splendid Victorian country house, that can make a trip to the "Great Northeast" a cultural, recreational and literary experience.

In fact, it's an ideal outing for families with young kids. The grounds of the estate have become Burholme Park, an attractive 70 acres of ball fields, picnic groves, woods and an excellent playground.

The house, sitting atop one of the few high hills in Philadelphia, contains splendidly furnished Victorian rooms, an independent

The incredibly ornate Chinese puppet theater.

free library and an interesting free museum that's well worth seeing.

An added bonus that seems to intrigue and fascinate all kids is a pet cemetery. The Ryersses were animal lovers of the mushy, sentimental variety. They buried their dearly departed horses, dogs, cats and rabbits near the mansion under standard tombstones. You can also see the four-footed friends in life. The family commissioned artists to paint portraits of proud doggies, including Fannie, Pinto and Jennie and of the rest of the managerie. These paintings decorate many rooms of the mansion.

The mansion was built in 1859 by Joseph Waln Ryerss, a prosperous Quaker merchant. The Waln part of the family were Quaker founding-fathers arriving with William Penn in 1682 aboard the ship Welcome. It appears that Joe Waln Ryerss married his two cousins: Susan Waln and her sister, Anne, after Susan's death.

Joseph, a power in the Orient trade, was also a railroad bigshot and made sure the railroad stopped at his estate. Ryerss Station, a block from the park, is still a commuter stop.

The mansion was built in the Italianate style with many large windows to insure cool breezes in the summer. (It was primarily a summer retreat.) There are also marble fireplaces in every room just in case it got too chilly. The mansion's crowning glory is a handsome roof cupola with stained-glass windows.

Wealthy 19th century folks – especially Philadelphia's merchant class – loved to collect exotic curios and artifacts from faraway places. And the Ryersses were particularly passionate about the mysterious Far East.

They put together a large and impressive Oriental collection: huge Chinese vases, an ivory chess set, hundreds of ivory figurines, wood carvings, brass objects, chests, incense burners. The Ryersses snared the entire contents of a Japanese temple and many Indian objects. Kids are always fascinated by a Tibetan urn made from a human skull. The most colorful and impressive object is a Chinese puppet theater.

A second-story museum room contains a variety of worldwide curios: souvenirs of the coronation of Britain's King Edward; Napoleonic-era art objects, display cases filled with carved canes, smoking pipes, knives, swords, beer steins, family china and glassware, 19th century figurines and knick-knacks.

The mansion's living and dining rooms are furnished in splendid Victorian items that should impress any antiques-buff.

Joseph Waln Ryerss left the estate to his son, Robert, a bachelor lawyer who continued the collecting tradition. Eight months before Robert died in 1896, at age 64 he married the family housekeeper, Mary Ann Reed. His will stated that the estate should be donated to the city after Mary's death, and he left money for its upkeep.

In 1910, Mary turned the property over to the city. The grounds became a park and the mansion housed the only city library in the Northeast for several decades. The library now operates independently of the city system. It serves about 3,000 cardholders living in the neighborhood. It's old-fashioned, comfortable, a pleasant place for rainy day reading.

The estate also provides some of the best sledding in the Northeast. On snowy days, hundreds of kids toting Flexible Flyers converge on the hill.

Burholme Park and the Ryerss Mansion are located at Cottman and Central avenues. Museum hours are limited to Saturdays and Sundays from 1 p.m. to 4 p.m. Phone: 685-0599

✳ ✳ ✳ ✳ ✳

The Ryerss family collected Oriental curios and arts.

The mansion also houses a public library.

The Ryerss Mansion is a Victorian masterpiece, museum and library.

*Founder Richard Allen is entombed
in the basement of Mother Bethel.*

Chapter 33

BLACK CHURCHES, HISTORIC AND EXOTIC

Even in the 19th century when only five percent of Philadelphia's population was African-American, the city had the largest black population of any Northern city. A great deal of black history was made in Philadelphia. The city remains an important center of African-American culture, a culture which often centers on the church. We visit three black churches, one historic and two surprising.

MOTHER BETHEL AME CHURCH

Sometimes a seemingly small event becomes an image forever frozen in historical memory: Ben Franklin flying a kite, General George Patton slapping a soldier.

One of those moments frozen in Philadelphia's historical memory occurred on a Sunday morning in 1787 at St. George's Methodist Episcopal Church, at 4th and Vine (still there and the world's oldest Methodist church). The church had allowed a small group of free blacks and slaves to worship, but their numbers grew, and the congregation's tolerance diminished. On the famous morning in 1787, more than 40 blacks were told to move to the gallery.

In one account of the incident, white church trustees rudely pulled kneeling black worshippers to their feet. The humiliated blacks left St. George's en masse, under the leadership of ex-slave and preacher Richard Allen, who declared, "We will trouble you no longer." This famous walkout might have been the first non-violent protest in African-American history.

Later the group purchased land on the corner of 6th and Lombard. The blacks then used a team of horses to haul an abandoned blacksmith shop to the site to serve as a church.

The all-black Bethel Church remained under Methodist control until 1816 when it, and a dozen other black churches, broke away and formed the African Methodist Episcopal Church. Richard Allen became the first bishop, and his church became "Mother Bethel," mother church of a new denomination.

A tremendous amount of black history surrounds Richard Allen and Mother Bethel AME Church.

The handsome sanctuary and huge organ of Mother Bethel.

For decades Mother Bethel AME was the heart and soul of Philadelphia's largest black neighborhood. The city's black Freemasonry movement was born there. All the great abolitionist leaders, including Frederick Douglass, spoke from its pulpit. It was the place for important mass meetings. It was a hiding place in the underground railroad.

Allen and his followers, working tirelessly as nurses and gravediggers, were heroes of the yellow fever epidemic of 1793, which killed 20,000 Philadelphians. During the War of 1812, Allen organized a black militia to defend the city in case of attack.

The present building dates to 1890 and is the fourth church to occupy the site – the oldest property in the nation continuously owned by blacks. There are members today who trace their families back to the church's first years, including a direct descendant of Richard Allen.

While not too impressive from the street, the church has a beautiful sanctuary, fine stained-glass windows and an impressive pipe organ.

Down in the basement is a marble and brick crypt containing the remains of Allen and his wife, Sarah. There's also a photo display of all the denomination's bishops. And Mother Bethel has a small, ecletic, museum collection that is extremely interesting.

Allen was a jack-of-all-trades – minister, carpenter, shoemaker, cooper, medical healer. Items of church furniture made by Allen, including the pulpit, a wood pillar and benches, are centerpieces of the museum.

Portraits of Richard and Sarah Allen.

Among the most interesting objects is a unique wood ballot box used to elect church officials. Members voted by placing marbles in a slot below a portrait of each candidate. The marbles were counted later to decide the winner. Both the early church furniture and the ballot box were lent to the Smithsonian Museum for a temporary exhibit.

Another fascinating artifact is an original poster printed by Boston abolitionists in 1851, warning blacks of slave catchers in the Boston area. There are several rifles associated with Allen's War of 1812 unit. Interesting documents include Allen's 17th century Bible and a "license to exhorte," or preach, signed by Allen in 1819. There's an old Sunday-school book and Sarah Allen's "X" on rent receipts.

The famous Philadelphia-born black artist Henry O. Tanner made a plaster cast of Richard and Sarah Allen that was to be cast in bronze as a church wall plaque. The memorial was never completed, but the cast is still on display.

The church provides enthusiastic guides who make a visit to this black shrine educational and rewarding.

Mother Bethel African Methodist Episcopal Church is at 6th and Lombard. Call ahead for tour information. Phone: 925-0616

PENNSYLVANIA DUTCH CHURCHES

The Pennsylvania Dutch, as we all know, arrived in the 17th and 18th centuries from Germany and Switzerland, fleeing persecution for their religious and pacifistic beliefs.

They dress "plain." The men grow beards. The women wear long dresses and bonnets. They're mostly farmers. They live in the country. They're white. Right?

Not entirely correct. Philadelphia is full of surprises and two big surprises can be found in the black neighborhoods of North Philadelphia. They are a predominantly black Mennonite con-

A rear view of the sanctury at Mother Bethel.

gregation and an entirely African-American Schwenkfelder church.

The Mennonite church should not be a complete surprise. Unlike the Amish, Mennonites are big on missionary work and proselytizing. Dressing "plain" is optional, and many Mennonites are urban dwellers.

In the mid-1930s Mennonites from Lancaster County arrived in North Philadelphia and built a small church. They started projects to aid poor blacks and launched a door-to-door proselytizing campaign. Their after-school and summer camp programs led to the conversion of a couple of dozen black children. In some cases these black Mennonite youngsters left the neighborhood to attend Mennonite schools in Lancaster County, where they did dress plain. Many of the core members of the church are senior citizens who became Mennonites as kids in North Philadelphia.

The small church is gone. The present church can be found inside a former Bell Telephone building converted by the Mennonites into a community center. The Diamond Street Community Center provides all sorts of neighbor-

The fourth Mother Bethel AME Church building on the same site.

hood services, including health care. Many on the staff are rural Mennonites performing a year of volunteer work in the city.

Pastor Charles Baynard is a black man raised on a Lancaster County farm. There was a Mennonite church near the family farm, and his parents joined mostly for the convenience. His wife is from North Philadelphia, one of those who left the neighborhood to attend Mennonite high school in Lancaster County.

There are a good number of white Mennonites in the congregation. Some are performing community service, others are city dwellers who enjoy the diversity of an interracial church.

The Schwenkfelder Church in the Strawberry Mansion section is a surprise. This is a very tiny sect whose history and beliefs are closely related to the Mennonites.

There are only 2,500 Schwenkfelders in the world. They have five churches – four in Montgomery County, where they settled in the middle of the 18th century and one in Strawberry Mansion.

The local church was built in 1898 to serve members of the church who drifted into the city. The neighborhood became predominantly Jewish in the late 1920s and predominantly black in the 1950s. But the church hung on, welcoming anyone who cared to join. There weren't many converts.

The simple but pretty First Schwenkfelder Church.

Only 15 or 20 worshippers came to the church in 1975 when Rev. T. Arnold Brooker, an ordained African Methodist Episcopal minister, agreed to take the pulpit. He visited the Schwenkfelder churches in the country and decided that despite its German roots, it was a rather mainstream Protestant faith. In fact, all Schwenkfelder ministers are graduates of other Protestant seminaries. So Brooker became a Schwenkfelder.

On "Rememberance Day," which marks the sect's arrival in Philadelphia in 1734, the black Schwenkfelders try singing a few German songs and eat the traditional meal of bread and apple butter.

Otherwise, worship is similar to other black churches, soulful and exuberant. Brooker says the other Schwenkfelders have been warm and welcoming. They visit from time-to-time and provide most of the financial support that keeps the small black church going. It's a simple but very pretty little wood church – a country church in the city. "It's like a picture postcard," says Rev. Brooker.

The Diamond Street Center and Mennonite Church is at 17th and Diamond streets. The First Philadelphia Schwenkfelder Church is at 2509 N. 30th Street.

✴ ✴ ✴ ✴ ✴

The modern Diamond Street Mennonite Church.

Ron Avery

MARILYN A. SHAPIRO

About the Author

Ron Avery is a Philadelphia native with 25 years experience in newspaper reporting and feature writing. He currently writes about local people and places for the Philadelphia Daily News.

He attended Philadelphia public schools and The Pennsylvania State University where he majored in history. Avery served as a Navy journalist before launching a newspaper career in 1966. Prior to the Daily News, Avery wrote for several Philadelphia suburban newspapers, including daily newspapers in Bucks County, Delaware County, Montgomery County and southern New Jersey.

"Philadelphia: Beyond the Liberty Bell," is his first book. It grew from his love of history, his special feel for the offbeat, and his intimate knowledge of Philadelphia and its suburbs.